WHAT PEOPLE ARE SAYING ABOUT *KNOW IT SECURITY*:

*"**KNOW IT Security** is a timely, easy, and fast read that is a must for senior managers in every large corporation to understand that good IT security is about business needs, physical security, human behaviors, and technology. Jim's approach to this important topic in this book is enlightened and enlightening."*

— *King Rogers, former Vice President of Assets Protection for Target Corporation*

*"**KNOW IT Security** is the most knowledge-packed, entertaining, and practical introduction to computer and network security that I have found. A must read for all corporate executives and managers."*

— Lynn McNulty, IT security consultant and long-time practitioner in the field.

*"Wow! How simple, and yet profound at the same time. **KNOW IT Security** provides the middle ground where techies and management can meet and agree. A fun, quick, and practical read."*

— Gretchen Ann Morris, CISSP, IT Security Expert

"Anyone interested in starting out in information security, risk management, or business executives in charge of running their companies should read this book. The novella story-telling approach makes comprehension of the key concepts: IT security introduction, business-based security strategies, and components to a total security approach, easier to newcomers."

— Lew Wagner, CPP, CISSP, Chief Information Security Officer, Clarian Health Partners, Inc.

*"**KNOW IT Security** should be required reading for every university student. It is also a great resource for both governmental and commercial managers."*

— Dr. Pam Collins, C.F.E., Professor Security Studies, Eastern Kentucky University

*"**KNOW IT Security** is entertaining and a quick read. It is a great first step for those new to, or newly responsible for, IT Security."*

— Christine Whalley, CISSP, IT Security Expert

*You can't make sound security decisions without understanding the issues. **KNOW IT Security** is a powerful and enabling book because it clearly explains, and puts into a business perspective, the key IT security concepts that managers and executives need to know to effectively manage their information security risks.*

— Ray Bernard, PSP, Security Consultant

*"**KNOW IT Security** is a must read for managers that have IT systems supporting their business. In non-technical terms, Jim effectively introduces key IT security concepts and technologies, so you can begin to make better security decisions."*

— Noelle Hardy, CISSP, CISM, Security Practitioner

"Jim combines a trip to an exotic island with an extensive evaluation of an online casino. The text is casual but the examples and points stay on the mind of the reader. By the time you finish the book, you realize that you have not only read an interesting story, but you learned dozens of pointers in the business of helping others secure their computers and networks!"

— Ron Lander, CPP, Ultrasafe Security Solutions

*Advances in technology have burdened both management and executives to be more technology savvy in order to take calculated risks and to make cost-effective decisions about securing the enterprise. **Know IT Security** provides great insights for building the required knowledge."*

— Juanita Koilpillai, Entrepreneur and Former Senior Program Director for Government Research at Symantec Corporation

KNOW
IT Security

SECURE IT SYSTEMS CASINO STYLE

James P. Litchko

KNOW BOOK PUBLISHING™

Kensington, MD
www.knowbookpublishing.com

KNOW IT Security
Secure IT Systems Casino Style

James P. Litchko

Published by:

Know Book Publishing
P.O. Box G
Kensington, MD 20895

publishing@knowbookpublishing.com
http://www.knowbookpublishing.com

Printed in the United States of America
First Edition

ISBN 0-9748845-0-2

LCCN 2004110405

Cover and Interior design by: Kristin L. Adolfson

Dedication

KNOW IT Security is dedicated to all individuals who taught me what IT security was really about. These leaders, experts, operators, interns, students and educators provided me with the IT security concepts, unique teaching techniques, and encouragement that allowed me to create this book, so others can learn from their efforts. Thanks to all who have touched my life in so many wonderful ways.

Foreword

I predict that ***KNOW IT Security*** is the book that will give business professionals the knowledge and confidence they need to manage their IT security.

This is the first book I have found that provides non-technical individuals with a quick, entertaining, and effective introduction on how to achieve successful IT security. In this book Jim Litchko presents and justifies all of the key concepts that will save management time and money, such as understanding that IT security solutions must support business requirements, that technology does not provide the total solution, and that you cannot achieve 100% security.

It is also impressive how he presents perceived complex IT security technologies, like firewalls and encryption. Not only does he effectively explain how they work, he equates them to real-life analogies. Complementing this with actual applications of the technology to solve a problem, the author effectively provides a non-threatening introduction to how security solutions work and what they can and cannot do for security.

I hope that you will enjoy reading this book as much as I did, and that you will be successful in managing your IT security.

— *Shirley A. Pierini, CPP, President of ASIS International and Vice President Corporate Security and Safety for Ameriquest*

Introduction

People don't learn to swim by being thrown into the middle of a deep pond. We all do much better wading in slowly, or playfully learning in the shallows.

As a new adjunct professor at Johns Hopkins University teaching business managers about computer and network security, I quickly learned that throwing the students into complex textbooks was not effective. It was better to have them read an entertaining novel related to the topic and use the novel's key points to introduce complex concepts and issues.

KNOW IT Security is a story written to allow executives, managers, and students to wade from the shallows into that deep pond we call "IT security". Loosely based on an actual security assessment that I participated in several years ago, this book provides the reader with a:

- low-tech introduction to IT system and Internet security threats, vulnerabilities, and countermeasures.
- business-based strategy to review IT systems for security needs.
- total security approach to securing IT systems using technical, physical, personnel, and procedural security methods.

My hope is that ***KNOW IT Security*** will give the reader an entertaining introduction to IT security basics, and increased confidence when dealing with security technologies and related issues.

— *Jim Litchko*

Contents

THE SCORE

The Score

Phil and Terry got onto the plane, happy to leave the heat of the sun, but disappointed to leave the calming serenity of the island's tropical atmosphere.

They settled into their seats, buckled up, and waited for the air conditioning to provide relief from the stifling heat. Phil turned to Terry and said, "You've been keeping score of the interesting things that you learned on this trip. What were the highlights?"

Terry thought a minute, referred to his PDA, and responded, "I learned:

- that three six-pack soda coolers can replace a $2,000 fireproof safe,
- that a one-time $4,000 crypto investment can save $16,000 a month,
- that IT security solutions are less than 20% technical solutions,
- to be ready for Blinding Flashes of the Obvious,
- that the best information technology security solutions are B.S., and
- to beware of the pepper sauce."

"Good, I'd say that you now have the knowledge needed to determine how much security is enough for any IT system," responded Phil.

"This was a very informative visit," agreed Terry, "and it has been worth the trip."

The Property

The Strip
The Biz
The Bar

The Strip

Phil took in the splendid view of the small tropical island as their propeller plane made its final approach on the runway.

Tap, tap, tap…

Terry, who accompanied him to provide in-depth technical support, sat actively tapping away on his new PDA. This gave Phil an idea. "Why don't you keep notes on anything you find interesting during this trip?"

"Cool," said Terry, as he noted it for future reference on the PDA.

Tap, tap, tap…

"What's cool is the fact that we're here to conduct a security assessment on an Internet gambling casino," Phil commented.

"I can't wait to see what this casino is going to look like," replied Terry.

"You know, I've been on the Las Vegas Strip before, but while we were circling the island, I saw nothing that looked like the casinos that I've seen before."

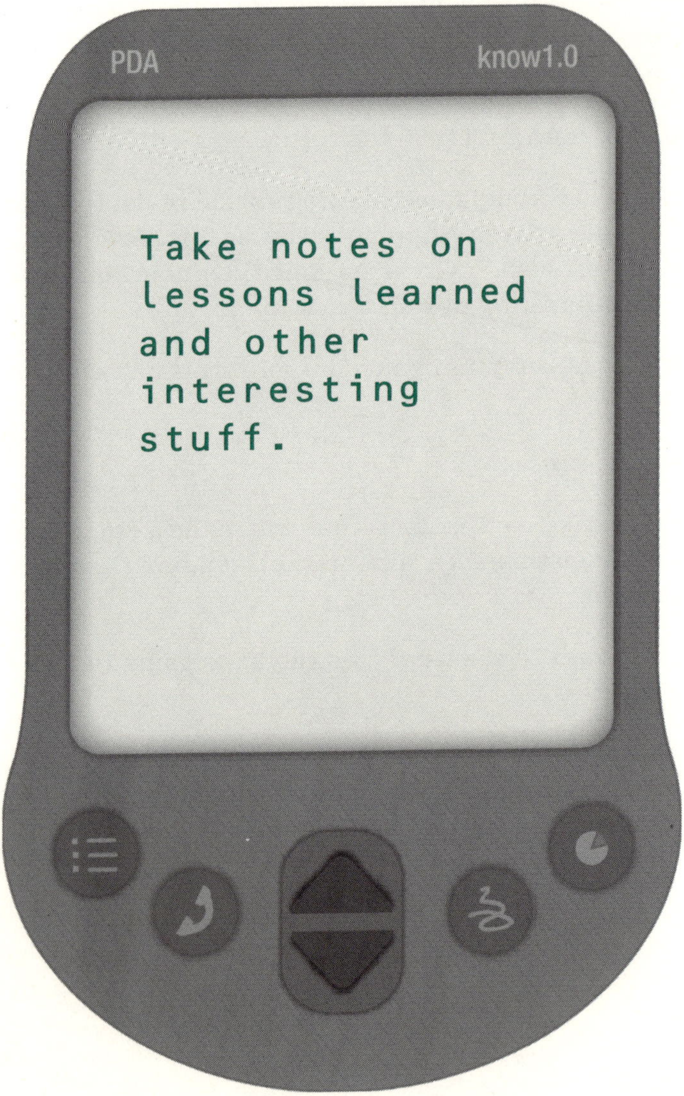
PDA
know1.0
Take notes on lessons learned and other interesting stuff.

After the plane landed and taxied to the gate, Phil and Terry exited the plane into a blast of hot, humid tropical air.

As they quickly passed through customs, Phil stopped and turned to the customs official. "Excuse me, we're here to meet Kris - "

The official interrupted, pointed, and said, "Here she comes."

"Welcome to our island in the middle of Paradise," Kris said warmly, "I'm Kris, the director of the operations at the casino."

"Good to meet you." Phil replied, "I'm Phil and this is Terry."

"Likewise," Kris said as she shook their hands.

"I wish all of our security assessments were in such a beautiful place," Phil said.

Kris chuckled. "Come with me and we'll get you a rental car." She led the way outside.

"Is that customs official a friend of yours?" Phil asked.

"Actually, he's married to one of my cousins. This is a very small island where everyone knows everyone else and their business."

Kris drove the newcomers across the island in Phil's rental car. The island's most prominent feature was a large volcano. Kris noticed Terry's nervous interest in this landmark. "Don't worry," she said, "it's been dormant for years. We get mild tremors, but that is all. What you need to worry about on this island is the local pepper sauce. It's hotter than any volcano and is never dormant!"

Tap, tap, tap…

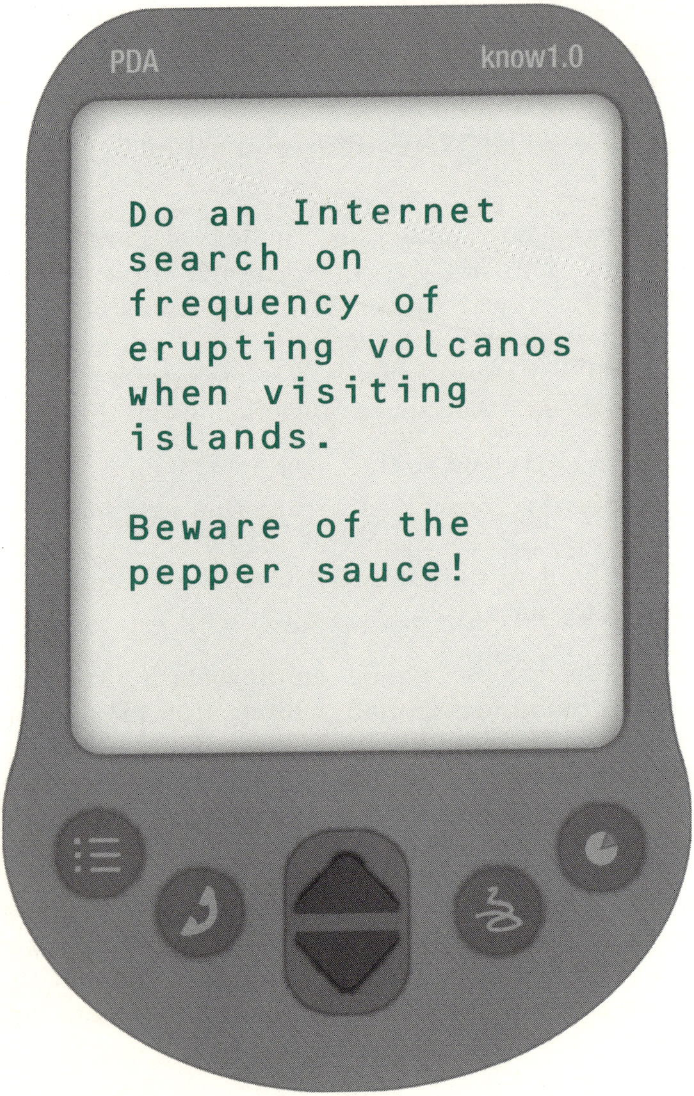
PDA
know1.0
Do an Internet search on frequency of erupting volcanos when visiting islands.
Beware of the pepper sauce!

After about fifteen minutes, they arrived at a one-story pastel-colored strip mall. This concrete, flat-roofed building held a bank, a restaurant, dime store, and grocery store. Located between the restaurant and the dime store was an unmarked pink unit with a heavily fortified door and windows.

"That's the casino?" Terry whispered to Phil.

"Not the Las Vegas Strip extravaganza that I was expecting," Phil whispered back.

Phil and Terry were expecting to walk into a noisy casino with the familiar one-armed bandits, blackjack and roulette tables, with waitresses immediately asking for their drink order. However the space revealed something much different.

They entered a room filled with desks, computers, wires, and calypso music. As their eyes finally adjusted from the strong sunlight to the dimly-lit room, they began to make out the inhabitants.

There were people typing on keyboards, and groups gathered around desks and whiteboards. The business uniform of the day was Bermuda shorts, tropical shirts, and sandals.

"Let me show you around," offered Kris.

"In this section, we have fourteen programmers who write the software that supports our website. Because of a time-critical delivery that we have to provide a client with this week, we also have eight contracted programmers helping them out.

We have twelve more graphic artists who design the game simulations that allow our clients, the Internet gamblers, to bet, play, win, and lose.

In this corner, we have the operational system that connects gamblers with the casinos. Sean is responsible for ensuring that those systems are up and running twenty-four/seven. He has been telling me all week about your attempts to scan and penetrate our systems over the Internet."

"We like to conduct our external system security testing a week prior to our visit, so that we don't waste any more of your time than we have to," Phil explained.

"Very efficient, I like that," turning to Terry she offered, "Sean will be showing you our system tomorrow."

"Tomorrow?" Phil asked, as it wasn't even dark yet.

"Well, it's almost three o'clock and I think it best that your first drive on the island be done during daylight," she stated.

Phil and Terry left the casino in their rental car. It was their first time driving in a country that drove on the left side of the road in a car with the steering on the right side of the car. To make things worse, Phil had to negotiate the car around the island's free-ranging goats, chickens, and steers on incredibly narrow roads that were also host to fast-moving tour buses and wide-load trucks.

For the first time since landing, Terry's mind was not on the volcano.

After coming to a full stop at their bungalow, Phil turned to Terry, "Remind me to go to the rental car company in the morning and buy full-coverage insurance for both us and the car."

Tap, tap, tap...

PDA
know1.0
Know your risks, vulnerabilities, and threats.
Always deploy countermeasures to help you reduce your losses.
Buy insurance.

The Biz

The next morning, Phil and Terry arrived at the casino after another challenging drive, this time with an upgraded insurance plan.

Kris greeted them at the door, “Good morning. So, how do you want to start?”

“Terry will take a look at your system, while you and I talk about your operations.”

“That sounds good to me. Sean, please help Terry. My office is this way,” she directed.

As they sat down, Kris turned directly to Phil and said, “I need you to understand that our business success depends on how good our security is, so please don’t sugar-coat what you find. If we have problems, I want to know what they are, and what my options are for fixing them.”

“Great, that will save us lots of time. Now, I have a couple questions for you.”

“I’m ready,” replied Kris.

"First off, in your own words, what is your business?"

"We design, establish, and maintain Internet gambling operations for physical casinos, so their customers, the cyber gamblers, can play, bet, win, and lose."

"Where are the casinos located?"

"One of the casinos is on the Island and the three others are located on several nearby islands."

"Who are the gamblers?"

"Like I said, anyone who wants to gamble. Typically, they're adults who are very impulsive and want to gamble immediately."

"And where are the gamblers?"

"The gamblers are all over the world and connect to our site using their Internet connections and browsers."

"What types of people are they?"

"Blue-collar workers, executives, managers, commercial, government, military, single, married, all genders, all races ...in other words anyone who has the money, time, computer, Internet connection, and desire."

"What are their capabilities?"

"They're your average computer user, with a new to five-year old personal computer. They know how to download software and use a browser, but we can expect nothing more technically."

"OK. So, how does the money get transferred?"

"The gamblers transfer money to a bank on the island. Because they want to gamble immediately, we let them play with one-third of their funds right away, but they can't retrieve any of their winnings or the balance until their money is received by our bank."

"Is there any sensitive information that they provide you with?"

"To some the fact that they are gambling is sensitive. The cash value of transactions, account numbers, bank names, and funds transfer codes are considered sensitive to most."

"Do the casinos have any unique requirements?"

"The casinos see all of their customers' information and transactions. They also want to have a real-time capability to watch the gamblers' actions while they are playing online. They're used to watching real players in real-time using their pit-bosses, guards, and surveillance cameras."

"How do you make your money?"

"The casinos let the gamblers play. We get a percentage of the money that their customers bet. There is no reduction in our percentage if the casino losses."

"From past personal experience, I know how the gamblers lose money. How can you and the casinos lose money?"

"In two ways: fraud and system outages. We figure the casinos lose between $10,000 and $50,000 for every hour that our operations are offline."

"Do you support any casinos that are competitors with each other?"

"Oh, yes. All four are competitors. We run different Internet sites for each, but they are all on the same computers here."

"So, how do you communicate with the casinos?"

"Well, usually we coordinate by phone. The computers are connected by leased lines. Their staff isn't very technical and casino management is not comfortable with connecting to the Internet, so e-mail is not an option."

"Leased lines between islands can be very expensive."

"You've got that right. On average our clients' monthly lease line charge is approximately $20,000 each."

"OK. Let's talk a little more about your specific operations. What does your internal organization look like?"

"We have three founders. I'm the director overseeing all aspects of the company, facilities, personnel, and finance. Tom runs client relations, sales, and marketing. He is visiting one of our supported casinos, so you will not be meeting him. Sean manages the programmers, graphic artists and system operations."

"How many computers support your whole operation?"

"We started in my garage with four. Today, we have about forty. Being a small operation, we tend to move the computers around so they are used in the most effective manner."

"How many network connections do you have to the Internet?"

"We currently have a low-speed connection and are now negotiating a separate high-speed connection, because of increasing demand. Customers do not like waiting for results, especially when money is involved."

"OK, that's all the questions. Let's go and look at your facility, so I can understand what the physical layout is like."

Phil walked around the inside, outside, and even visited the restaurant and dime store. During the tour, Phil stopped and talked with several employees to get an idea of their overall security awareness levels.

In the middle of the afternoon, Phil, Kris and Terry gathered near the front door.

"We're going to go and compare our notes," Phil said. "Tomorrow, we'll provide you with what we found, and give you a list of our security concerns and recommendations."

With an inquisitive look, Kris asked, "But you haven't asked me any questions about our security, like firewalls, encryption, passwords, anti-virus protection, or backups."

"Trust me. I've got everything I need from your answers about your business, operations, goals, your clients' capabilities and expectations, and the casinos' culture and capabilities. Combine that with what Terry has gathered, and we'll know what your security status is and what it should look like."

Tap, tap, tap…

"You see, I've learned that people are more comfortable talking about what they created than they are talking about their security."

Kris looked puzzled at first and then realized what Phil had done. "You smooth-talked me into spilling my guts about the most sensitive elements of my system! Now I'm really glad we signed a non-disclosure agreement."

"Painless wasn't it?"

"I'm looking forward to what you're going to do next," Kris said.

"Speaking of which, tomorrow I'll need a step ladder."

She gave Phil another puzzled look, but agreed.

"See you tomorrow."

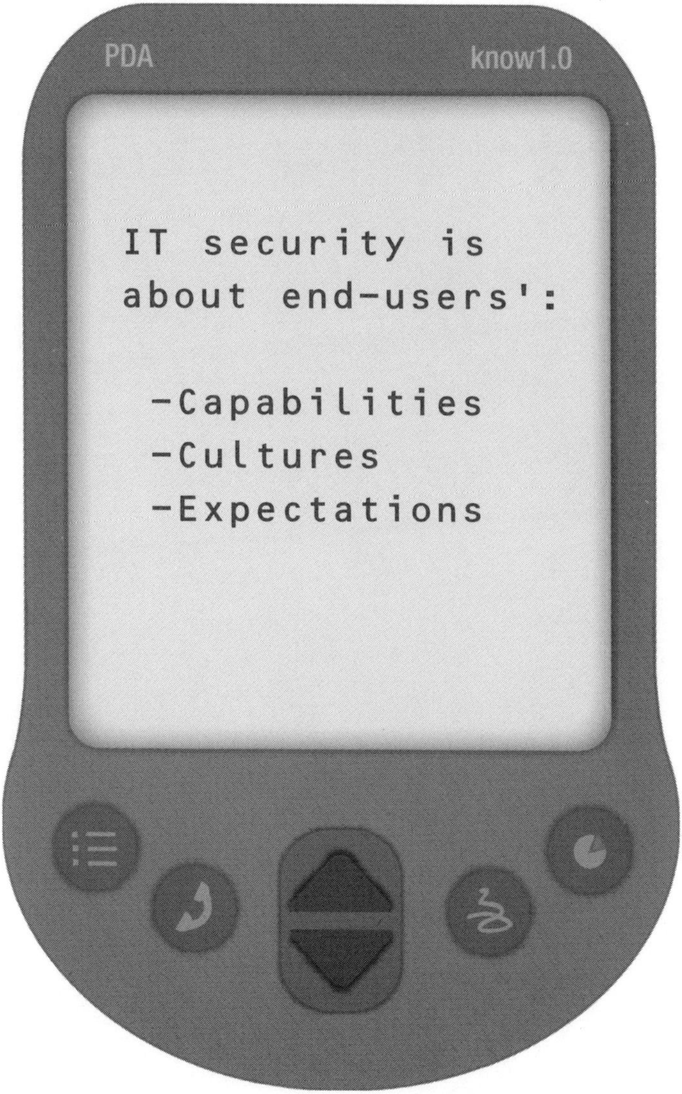
PDA
know1.0
IT security is
about end-users':
-Capabilities
-Cultures
-Expectations

The Bar

Late in the afternoon, Phil and Terry ate a black beans and rice dinner at the local "meat-on-a-stick" restaurant. Cautiously, they tried the pepper sauce.

Tap, tap, tap…

PDA
know1.0
Thank Kris for
the pepper sauce
warning.

Their hunger satisfied, they retreated to a local bar on the beach to review their findings from the casino while sampling a few of the local drinks.

They noticed the bar was basically a large wooden deck with plastic chairs, small round tables, and a large box from which drinks where served.

The box was eight feet long, three feet high, and two feet deep. The back had cabinets to store the bar's glasses, mixes, ice, sodas, beer, napkins, bar utensils, and cash register. The top served as a counter top for mixing the drinks. There was a long piece of angled iron placed across the cabinet doors, with locks at both ends to secure the bar at closing. These security measures were augmented by a very large dog chained to an eye-hook in the center of the cabinets.

Seated and served, Phil started, "That bar is a perfect example of the best solution for a specific need: efficient, effective, user-acceptable, practical, and secure."

"Your basic latch, lock, and large dog security," Terry responded.

"Yes, but appropriate and effective," Phil replied. "So, what did you find at the casino?"

"Their system is the typical pre-security assessed system. The firewall software is several versions old, passwords are weak, multiple unnecessary router ports are open, there's a modem backdoor for remote administration of the website, the original operating system password is active, the anti-virus signatures were last updated two weeks ago, and they are using installation defaults on most of their commercial software.

"Basically, any one of the forty people on-site can change anything on the system. And with the modem, the port 80 situation, and the out-of-date firewall, anyone on the outside with some hacker sense and tools can, too."

"By **port 80**, you mean the router and firewall configuration that connects the Internet directly to internal software applications?" confirmed Phil.

"Correct. In this case the software applications are the casino games and the transaction programs."

"Got it." responded Phil.

Terry continued, "A lot of people think that a firewall provides total protection from Internet threats. What they don't understand is that when they allow access to internal programs through port 80 they have to ensure these programs and supporting computer systems are very secure or anyone could hack in and take over their system," Phil commented.

"It's kind of like having a guard in an apartment complex monitoring who is coming in and out, but not having anyone protect the security, maintenance, boiler, or air conditioning rooms," added Terry.

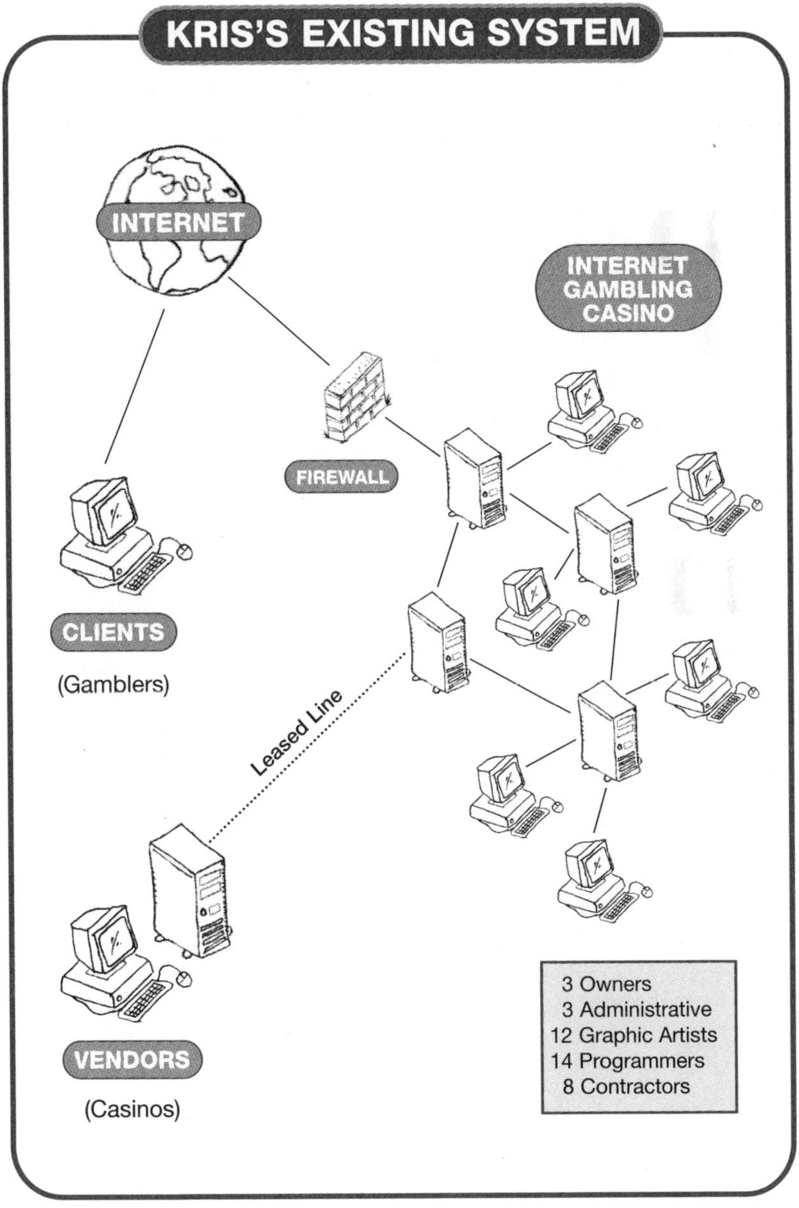
KRIS'S EXISTING SYSTEM
INTERNET
INTERNET GAMBLING CASINO
FIREWALL
CLIENTS
(Gamblers)
Leased Line
VENDORS
(Casinos)
3 Owners
3 Administrative
12 Graphic Artists
14 Programmers
8 Contractors

Phil moved the conversation forward, "We will have to recommend some strong testing and configuration control measures for those game and transaction programs. What else did you find?"

"They also have an uninterrupted power supply, or UPS that should provide enough power to allow them to smoothly shut the system down if they have a power failure."

"Good job."

Suddenly, there was a loud thump and the deck shook violently. Terry cringed and stole a quick glance at the volcano. There was no change. Quickly looking around the bar, Phil noticed that a pickup truck filled with speakers and audio equipment had just backed into the deck.

"Tonight's entertainment," announced the Phil.

"How did your talk with Kris go?" asked Terry.

"Well, Kris is very interested in hearing our findings and recommendations, which is a good thing. We're here because the Board of Directors and potential investors requested that a third-party give them a professional opinion on their security.

"Better yet, she understands that she cannot afford to make her system 100% secure, and that there will still be residual risks when all is done.

"No B.S. and no sugar-coating the facts is what she wants, but **B.S.** is what she is going to get: **Business-based Security.**"

"What?" asked Terry, looking a bit baffled.

"I'm sorry. When I conduct a security assessment I use a **business approach**. During the interview with the owner, I question them about their business, not their security. It makes the effort a lot less confrontational. It also allows us to base our security recommendations on their **business requirements**, not just security. I find that management relates to facts easier then fear. It's a much better approach then using the typical **'fear, uncertainty and doubt'** or **'FUD'** approach that most people use to scare the client into accepting their security solutions."

Tap, tap, tap…

Grabbing a couple of cocktail napkins and a pen, Phil continued, "Let's order another couple of drinks and draw what Kris' system should look like."

Calypso music, punctuated by crashing waves, a couple more drinks, and a bowl of green peanuts and raisins got their creative juices flowing. Phil and Terry hunched over several cocktail napkins and sketched a system that was built with the business, users, and security in mind.

Together they sought to create a system that was as effective, efficient, user-acceptable, practical, and secure as the minimal design of the bar at the end of the deck. Five cocktail napkins later, they completed their task and the customers at the bar were in full party mode.

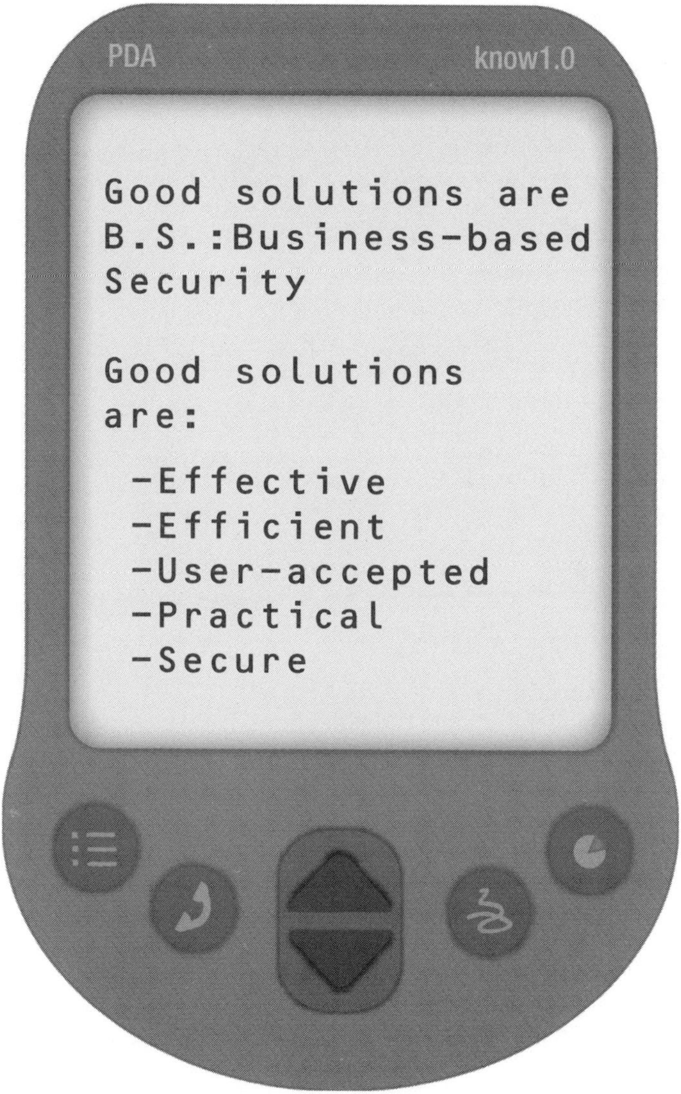
PDA
know1.0
Good solutions are B.S.:Business-based Security
Good solutions are:
-Effective
-Efficient
-User-accepted
-Practical
-Secure

The Casino

The Cocktail Napkins
The Odds
The Players

The Cocktail Napkins

The next morning, Phil and Terry chased chickens from the front of the car, shooed the wild goat from the car's roof, and wiped a layer of gray dust from the top surfaces.

As they entered the casino, they were greeted by Kris and Sean.

"Good morning, how are you feeling? Did you eat and sleep well?"

"Very well to all questions, thank you."

"We want to thank you for warning us about the power of the pepper sauce," commented Terry.

"We like hot food, but only in moderation," added Phil.

"We like to inform our visitors what the potential threats are. It's your responsibility to determine if you are willing to take the risk," Kris explained with a smile.

"How did you like the bar?" asked Sean.

"How did you know we were there?"

"This is a small island, remember?" Kris reminded Phil.

"You had mentioned that before."

"What's your plan for today?" Sean asked.

"We're going to review with you what we think your system should look like from a business and security perspective."

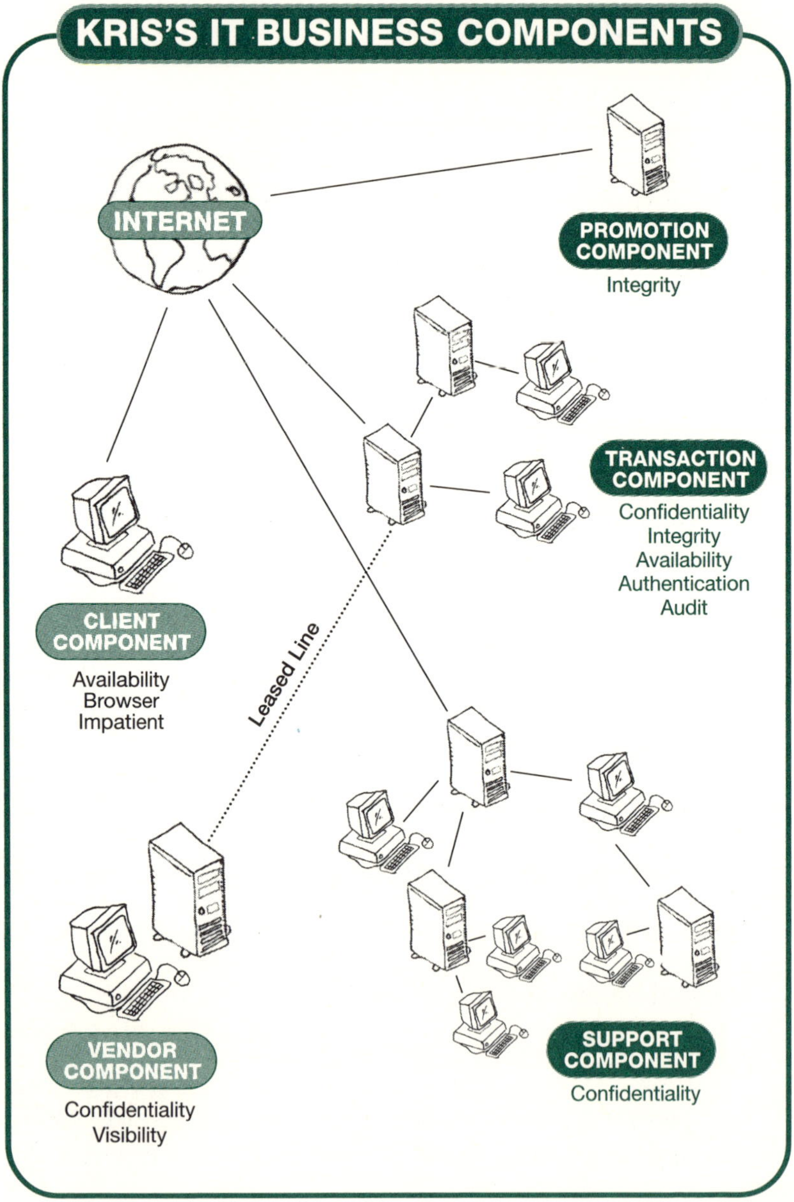
KRIS'S IT BUSINESS COMPONENTS
INTERNET
PROMOTION COMPONENT
Integrity
TRANSACTION COMPONENT
Confidentiality
Integrity
Availability
Authentication
Audit
CLIENT COMPONENT
Availability
Browser
Impatient
Leased Line
VENDOR COMPONENT
Confidentiality
Visibility
SUPPORT COMPONENT
Confidentiality

That morning, Phil had transferred the napkin drawings to a large piece of flip-chart paper so everyone could see the drawings and he could add notes as they talked during the review.

Laying the paper face down on the table, Phil began the discussion, "Now, what I'm going to show you is a functional drawing of your system that uses the business and technical information that we collected yesterday. Remember, this is a *functional* drawing, not a detailed drawing. We're not going to compare this with what you have, but with what your needs are. OK?"

They all nodded in agreement.

Phil flipped over the paper, so they could see the drawing.

He allowed them time to absorb the various notes, lines, and figures, so they could get their bearings.

"What you see here is that basically your business has five functional components: Promotion, Transaction, Support, Clients, and Vendors.

At this location, you have the Promotion, Transaction, and Support components. The Client components, the gamblers, are connected via the Internet and the Vendor components, the casinos, are connected via leased lines."

"That's correct," Kris concurred.

"I'll start with the business functions first, because I believe that security is deployed for business reasons first and for security reasons second."

Kris and Sean looked at each other with puzzled expressions.

"Let me explain, and I think you'll understand what I mean," he continued, "Each of these functional areas has specific business and security requirements. The Promotion component is one of the easier ones, so I'll start there.

"The **Promotion component** is where you have the website advertising for the casinos' games and where a potential customer learns about your services.

"The only security requirement here is to maintain the integrity or accuracy of the website. We need to ensure that no one can change the site. The common attacks on website integrity are called graffiti and lead referral attacks.

"A **graffiti attack** is where someone changes the content of the site, as a protest or prank, like changing the 'Department of Justice' site to read 'The Department of Injustice'.

"The **lead referral attack** is an industrial espionage and fraud technique. This is when some of the website links are changed to divert potential customers to other sites.

"In your case, the gambler clicks on your 'I want to play' button and is transferred to one of your competitors' gambling sites. Most customers are impulse buyers and they don't take the time to ensure that they are buying from the original site.

"Another lead referral attack is to change the vendor or bank website's login link to an unauthorized site that looks like the normal login site.

"You enter your login name and password, and in return you get a 'login error, please try again' response. When you try to login again, you have been routed back to the real login site, where you finally login successfully, and begin to play with your money.

"Later the unauthorized individual uses your login name and password to log into your account and play or withdraw your money.

"Any questions?" asked Phil.

Everyone shook their head.

"Now you don't want your potential customers logging into your Promotion component, because that doesn't make good business sense. No one wants to spend their time registering for a password just to see your ads. If you make them register, they will just go to one of your competitors who doesn't require them to login."

Tap, tap, tap…

"What about remote management of the site?" Sean asked.

"I strongly recommend that you do not authorize anyone to remotely login over the Internet to administer this component. From our talks yesterday, nothing you said told me that you needed to change your website in a hurry. Besides, this is a small island, so why risk compromising the site for the minor inconvenience of a short drive?"

"You're right. No remote logins," responded Kris.

Tap, tap, tap…

"The next on-site component is the **Transaction component**. It's the most critical component of the three at your location, since this is where your revenue-generating services are.

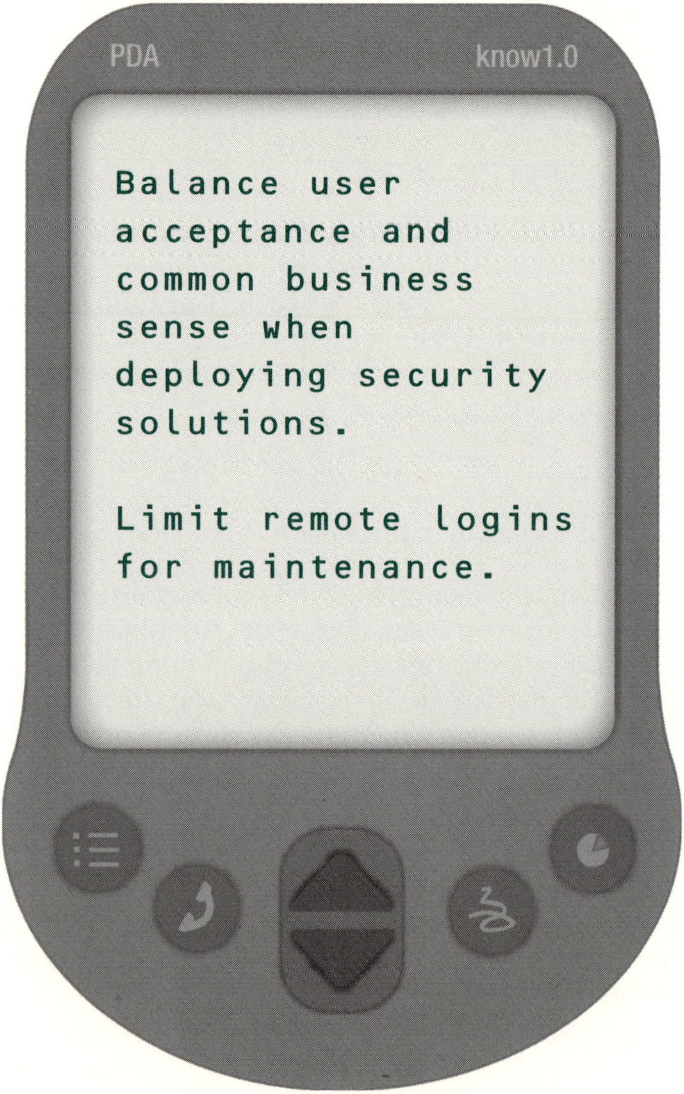

Balance user acceptance and common business sense when deploying security solutions.

Limit remote logins for maintenance.

"Essentially this is your store and bank, so there are many security requirements here: confidentiality, integrity, availability, authentication, and audit.

"**Confidentiality** is required because customers want their privacy maintained. Also, some of the casinos that you represent are competitors with each other, and their client lists are pure gold to another competitor's sales force, because these clients are all qualified leads.

"**Integrity** is obvious, because you're playing with money. If someone adds or removes a zero to any number, it has a major impact on your bottom line.

"Of these, **Availability** is one of the most critical. Yesterday, Kris said that your casinos lose $10,000 to $50,000 every hour that your gambling services are not online. This is different from your Promotion component, which could be down for days and result in minimal impact on your operations.

"**Authentication** is necessary to ensure that clients can only use and see their own accounts, and that the casinos can only have access to their own clients' data.

"Finally, you want to conduct **Audits** on the system to ensure that everything is working correctly and that no fraudulent activities are being conducted."

"Confidentiality, integrity, availability, authentication, and audit are the **'CIAAA'** security functions that you wrote about in your recent Internet security article," stated Kris.

"That's right," concurred Phil.

Tap, tap, tap…

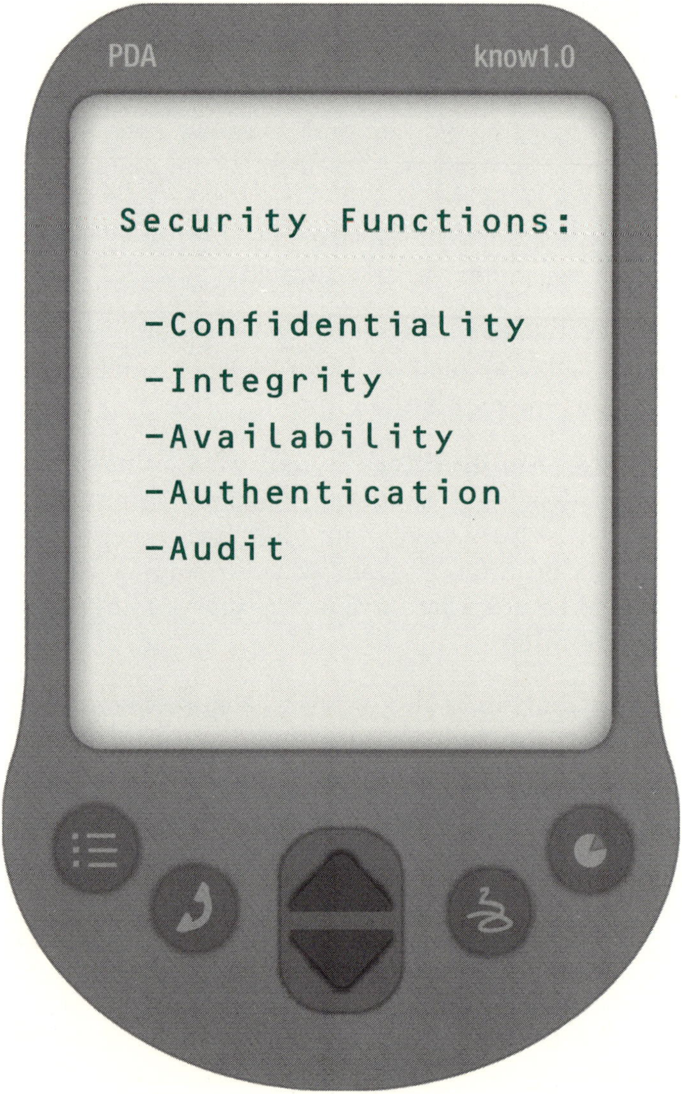
PDA
know1.0
Security Functions:
-Confidentiality
-Integrity
-Availability
-Authentication
-Audit

"Now, the **Support component** is where your contractors, programmers and graphic artists work. The requirements here are less strict. The key requirement here is confidentiality. This group develops the software used by the Transaction and Promotion components. This software needs to be protected from being seen or changed by outsiders.

"Why? Because it costs you a lot of corporate resources to design and develop your unique software applications that makes your website more popular then your competitors, so they should be viewed as intellectual property and protected. Agreed?"

Kris and Sean agreed.

"That pretty much covers the in-house systems' requirements. Did I miss anything?"

Phil glanced at the group and noticed that Kris looked troubled.

"Did I say anything that upset you?"

"No, it's just that this is the first time I've seen our system on a piece of paper and I'm surprised at how obvious everything is. I'm asking myself, why didn't I see this before?"

Phil smiled. "Your reaction is typical for people growing a new business.

I call this a **BFO** moment: a **Blinding Flash of the Obvious**."

Tap, tap, tap…

"You shouldn't be embarrassed by this. Remember you've been focused on growing your business, building a system that supports perceived and real customer needs, hiring and managing personnel, getting finances, selling, and marketing. You just haven't had the time to step back and give it a fresh look."

Tap, tap, tap...

Kris sighed. "Thank you. Just seeing this drawing has me re-evaluating some of my physical, organizational, and personnel decisions. As far as I'm concerned, you've earned your fee already."

"Good. While you two are re-evaluating, Terry and I will get us some more coffee."

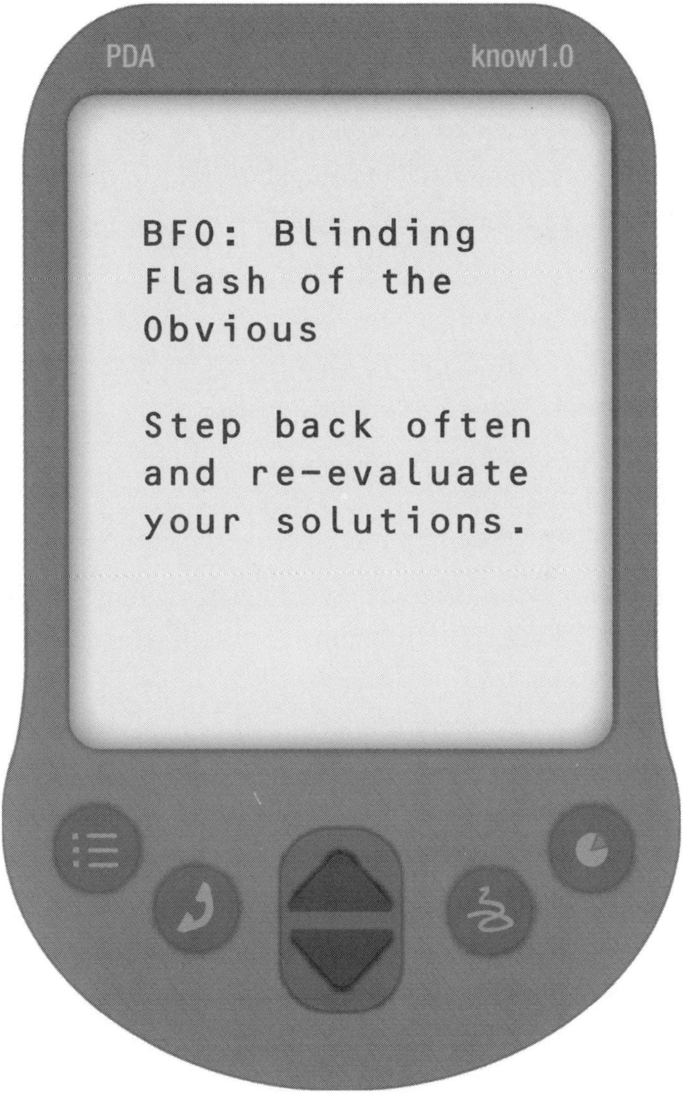
PDA
know1.0
BFO: Blinding Flash of the Obvious
Step back often and re-evaluate your solutions.

The Odds

Phil and Terry distributed the coffee among the group. As they were passing around the cups, Kris and Sean looked up from the drawing with large eyes and wide smiles.

"Phil, look at what we discovered! Simply by reconfiguring our system like you've drawn it here, we've increased security and decreased the systems' overall maintenance requirements," Kris exclaimed.

"Explain," Phil replied, leaning forward with interest. Phil knew it was important for clients to own their system's security solutions, so one of his tactics was to provide them with the concepts and the drawing, so they could come to their own conclusions and solutions. Allowing them to tell him what they learned on their own and giving them credit for solving the problems, was the final step toward their gaining total ownership of their solutions. He noticed that Terry recognized what he was doing as he watched him type into his PDA.

Tap, tap, tap…

Get users' ownership for solutions by leading them to discover their solutions.

Sean continued, "Knowing that we don't have to secure all computers with the same level of security provides us with major savings when we buy our security solutions. Only yesterday we were thinking that we had to secure all of the computers the same. How ridiculous!"

"Actually, that's what most people think. In fact, in the 1980's, many people were promoting it. So don't feel bad about your initial conclusions."

"Really?" Sean said, surprised, "We also identified how to reduce our greatest threat: our insiders."

"Today we have forty employees and contractors that can change anything in the system. That's a major threat," Kris announced.

Tap, tap, tap…

"By breaking-up the system like you've shown here, we can reduce the insider threat from a potential of forty people to only three, a risk reduction of at least twelve to one," added Sean.

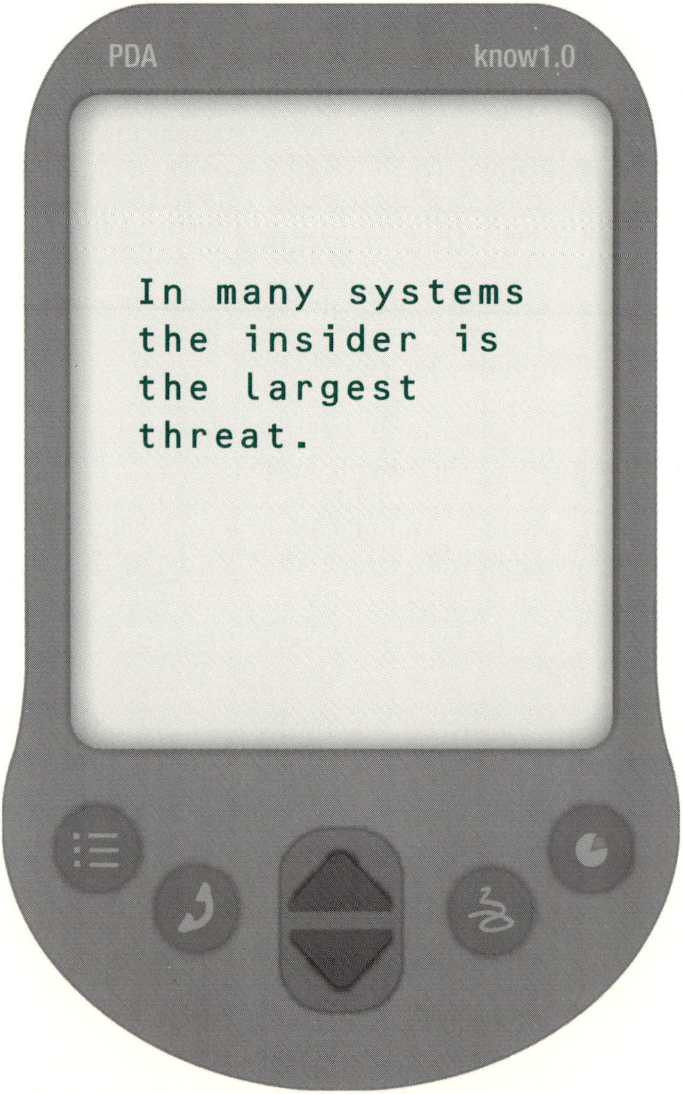
PDA
know1.0
In many systems the insider is the largest threat.

"Because the Promotion and Transaction components are the most critical to the success of the business, we just concluded that those systems should be physically separated from the Support component and that only three individuals should have access to those two systems," added Kris.

"Further, we decided to reduce the risk even more by giving physical access to our three most trusted employees," added Sean.

"How will you decide who are the three most trusted?" asked Phil.

"Well, we immediately ruled out the contractors, because we don't know their backgrounds and they have no obligation to the company," Kris explained, "so that left us with thirty-two employees."

"We wouldn't have hired them if we didn't trust them, so we had to develop other criteria that demonstrate who is the most loyal and committed to the success of our operation," said Sean.

"Our conclusion was to choose the three major stockholders: Sean, Tom, and I." Kris identified, "Who else has more to lose if the security fails?"

Tap, tap, tap…

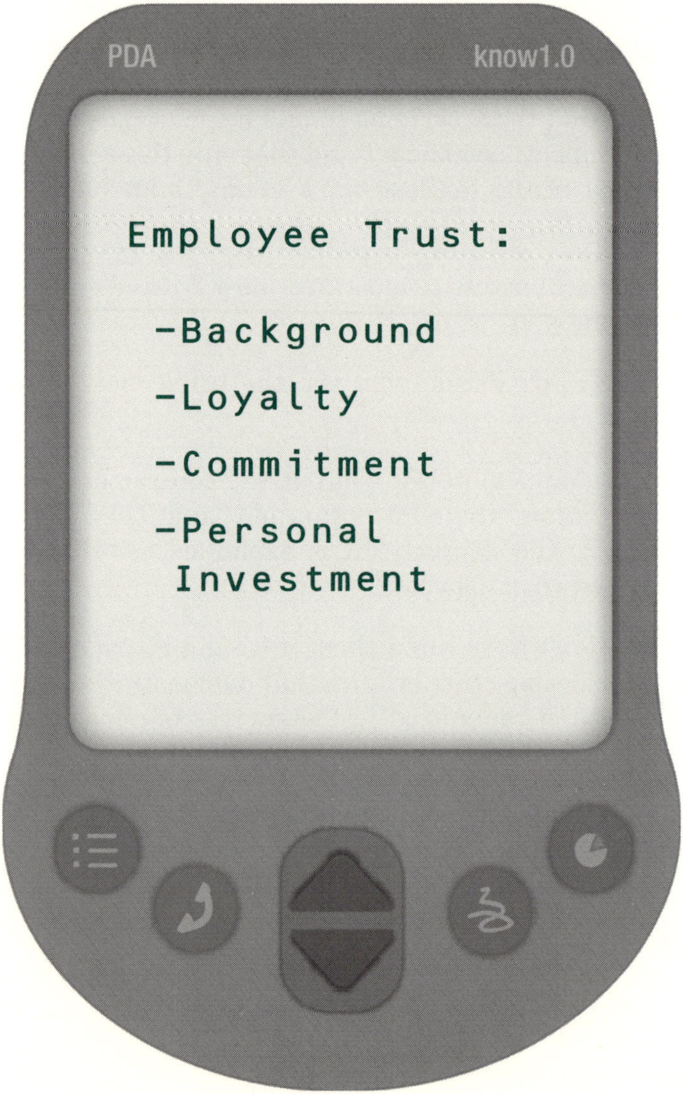
PDA
know1.0
Employee Trust:
-Background
-Loyalty
-Commitment
-Personal Investment

Phil was impressed with how fast they came to their conclusions, so he said, "Now that's a good solution: practical, realistic, efficient, and cost-effective. You both are to be congratulated."

Tap, tap, tap…

"Thank you, but we're not finished. We've found additional savings related to maintaining configuration control. You know ensuring that vendor software updates are done and that any changes to the hardware and software have security and functionality tests conducted, are approved, and documented," Kris said.

"As you know, a major key to reducing design vulnerabilities is to have strong control over the software and hardware." Sean continued, "Now here is where the savings comes from. You see, originally we thought that we had to apply strong configuration control to all of our computers, a very costly decision."

Sean continued, "But with this new view of our system we only need to put strong configuration controls on the Promotion and the Transaction computers. With only three people having access to those computers, that makes configuration control easier."

"Great! What about the Support component?" Phil asked.

Sean replied, "The Support component systems are being used by the most creative employees in our company. Asking them to get permission before they can make changes to their computer configurations, and to document the changes, would result in never-ending expense, frustration, and increased employee turnover."

"Our alternative is that we'll just have to do some strong testing of any software on a stand-alone system prior to moving it to the Promotion and Transaction components. We'll move the software using physical media, not a direct connection between the systems," Sean concluded.

"Also, we'll schedule the upgrades only during periods when the clients' use of the systems are the lowest, thus reducing the loss potential if something goes wrong," added Kris.

"Excellent solutions," Phil commended.

Tap, tap, tap…

"We're progressing very well," Phil noted.

IT Security is also about personnel, physical, and procedural considerations.

All IT systems do not need the same level of security.

The Players

"Now let's talk about the outsiders," Phil started, "Like many Internet businesses, you are providing an interface so your customers can get to the services and products of your vendors. In your case, you are connecting clients to the vendors' or international gamblers to the casinos around the Caribbean.

"The **Vendor component** functions are based on the *culture* of their businesses and their attitudes about the Internet. Basically, the casinos' needs are confidentiality and visibility, or in standard security terms the latter is called availability.

"Confidentially is pretty obvious, they don't want their operations revealed to competitors.

"Visibility is important because the physical casinos are used to having constant visibility on their tables and machines using the dealers, pit bosses, security personnel and video surveillance techniques. They are accustomed to watching every card and chip played."

"You truly understand the casino's culture," commented Kris.

"Thank you. Now the **Client component** is the most demanding of all the functional components, because it consists of your customers. Their needs must be accommodated or they'll go to one of the many other competing Internet casino sites.

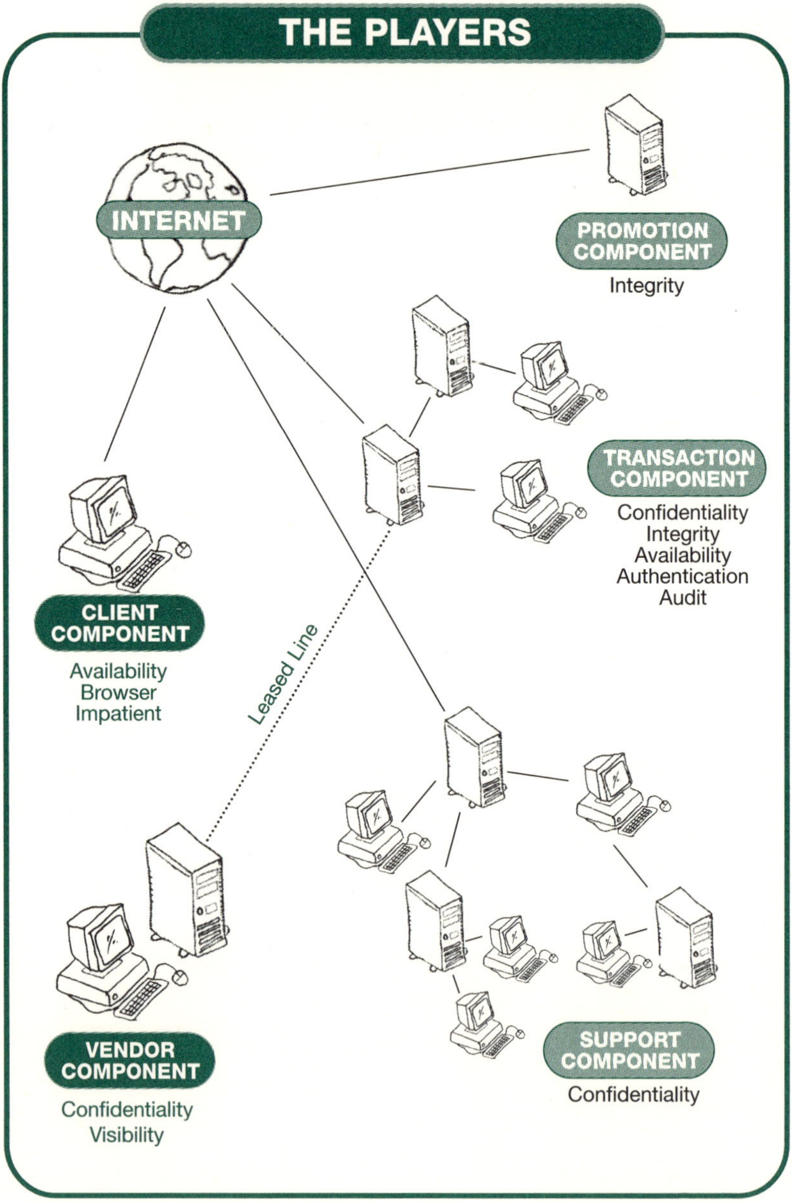
THE PLAYERS
INTERNET
PROMOTION COMPONENT
Integrity
TRANSACTION COMPONENT
Confidentiality
Integrity
Availability
Authentication
Audit
CLIENT COMPONENT
Availability
Browser
Impatient
Leased Line
VENDOR COMPONENT
Confidentiality
Visibility
SUPPORT COMPONENT
Confidentiality

"Their impulsive nature makes them want to gamble immediately. You know this because you allow for it in your current operations. You're letting them play with one-third of the money that they say they are transferring to your bank and giving them several days to complete the entire transfer.

"When deciding on the best authentication mechanism we cannot expect them to wait for something to come in the mail, like a token or smart card, before they can play.

"But they do want some type of security, like a login screen and password, because they're playing with their money, so they want to feel that their investment is being protected. Their *expectation* is that you are going to protect their money and personal information.

"Finally, the games must work within the *capabilities* of their system and what they're already comfortable with, like their browser. We cannot assume that they have the technical *ability* or *desire* to install new software or hardware."

Tap, tap, tap…

"Good! We have completed a very important step today. By identifying who can see and modify what, which systems are critical, and who is responsible, you have clarified the security policy for your system. A complete and accurate security policy is needed to ensure that the security solutions are deployed correctly."

Tap, tap, tap…

"This is the perfect time to break. Sean and I have an important meeting with our insurance representative this afternoon, so we will have to pick this up again tomorrow," Kris informed them.

"No problem. We'll draft the key elements of a security policy for you, so you can review them and approve it. Terry, let's get some lunch."

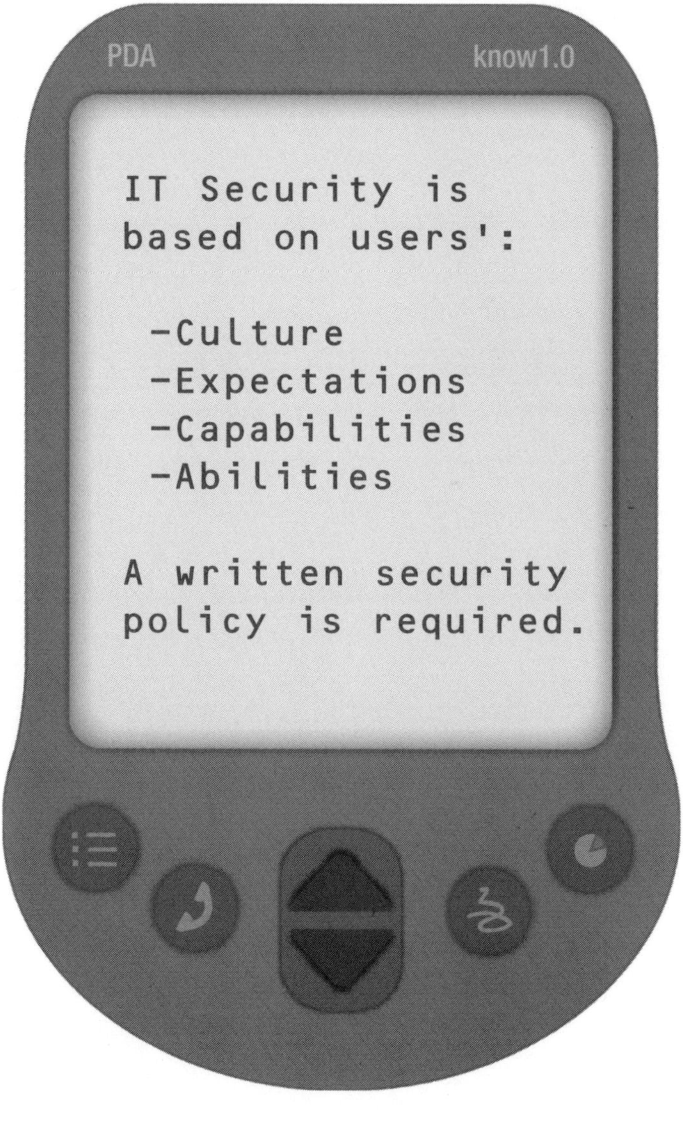
PDA
know1.0
IT Security is based on users':
-Culture
-Expectations
-Capabilities
-Abilities
A written security policy is required.

The Facilities

The Glitz
The Cashier Cage
The Secure Tubes

The Glitz

The next morning after completing their ritual of removing the chickens, goat, and dust from the car and driving to the casino, they all gathered at the conference room table. Kris turned to Phil, “The suspense is killing us, what’s the ladder for?”

“First, tell me why people are on the roof with shovels?” Phil asked.

“They’re shoveling off the volcanic ash that is coming from the erupting volcano two islands down the chain,” informed Kris.

Startled, Terry blurted, “What? That’s volcanic ash that we’re washing off of our car every morning?”

“We thought you knew,” said Sean.

“You wanted to know about the ladder?” Phil interjected to change the subject.

Everyone nodded in agreement. Terry slowly shook his head and mumbled to himself.

“All of our computers are at eye-level or below, so why do you need a ladder?” Sean added.

Phil began, “Well, as you know, casinos install glitz and glamour to focus your attention on their games and to draw it away from the ugly pipes and ventilation systems in the ceilings, and most importantly the surveillance cameras.

“When I first got here I was impressed with your window and door security, but being suspicious by nature, I looked up and down to see what other potential security weaknesses exist.”

"Like what?" asked Sean.

"Get me the ladder and I'll show you."

They brought in the ladder. Phil leaned it against the wall adjacent to the dime store and said, "I noticed that you have no internal motion detectors."

"We have glass-break and unauthorized opening detection alarms on the windows and doors, so that covers any potential entries," Kris explained, "Why should we install internal motion detectors?"

"You need them because the walls between you and the dime store do not go all the way to the roof." At the top of the ladder, Phil pushed the false ceiling tile up and showed them the two-foot gap between the wall and the building's roof.

They all stood starring with dropped jaws at the gap. "If you had a raised floor, I wouldn't have needed the ladder to prove my point," Phil added.

Tap, tap, tap…

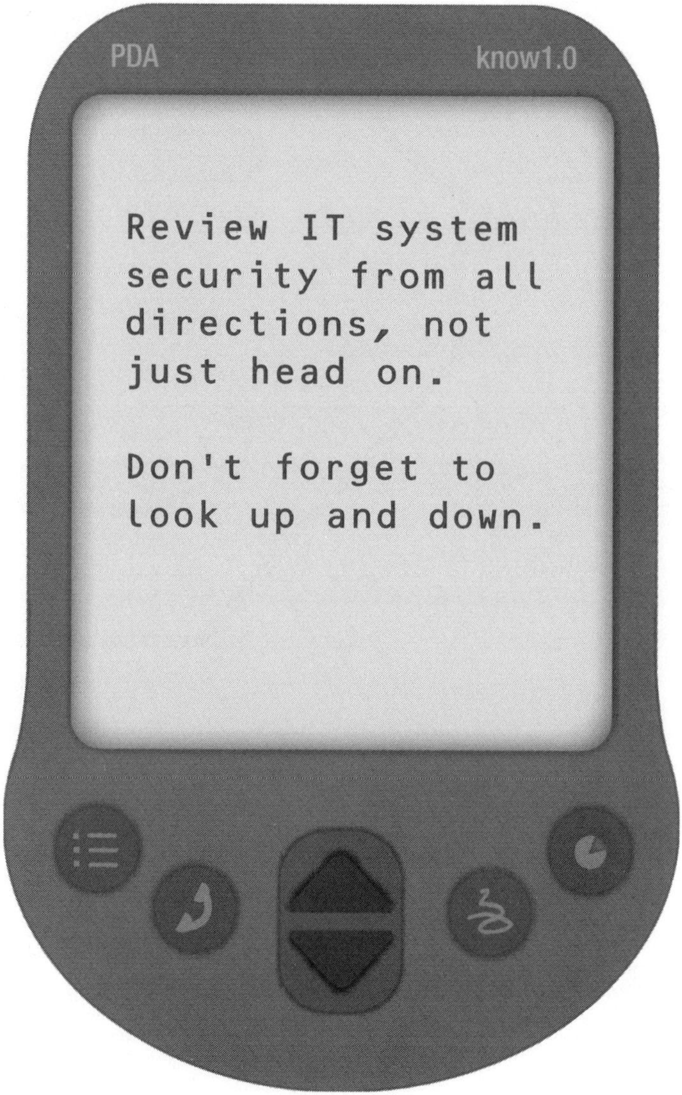
PDA
know1.0
Review IT system security from all directions, not just head on.
Don't forget to look up and down.

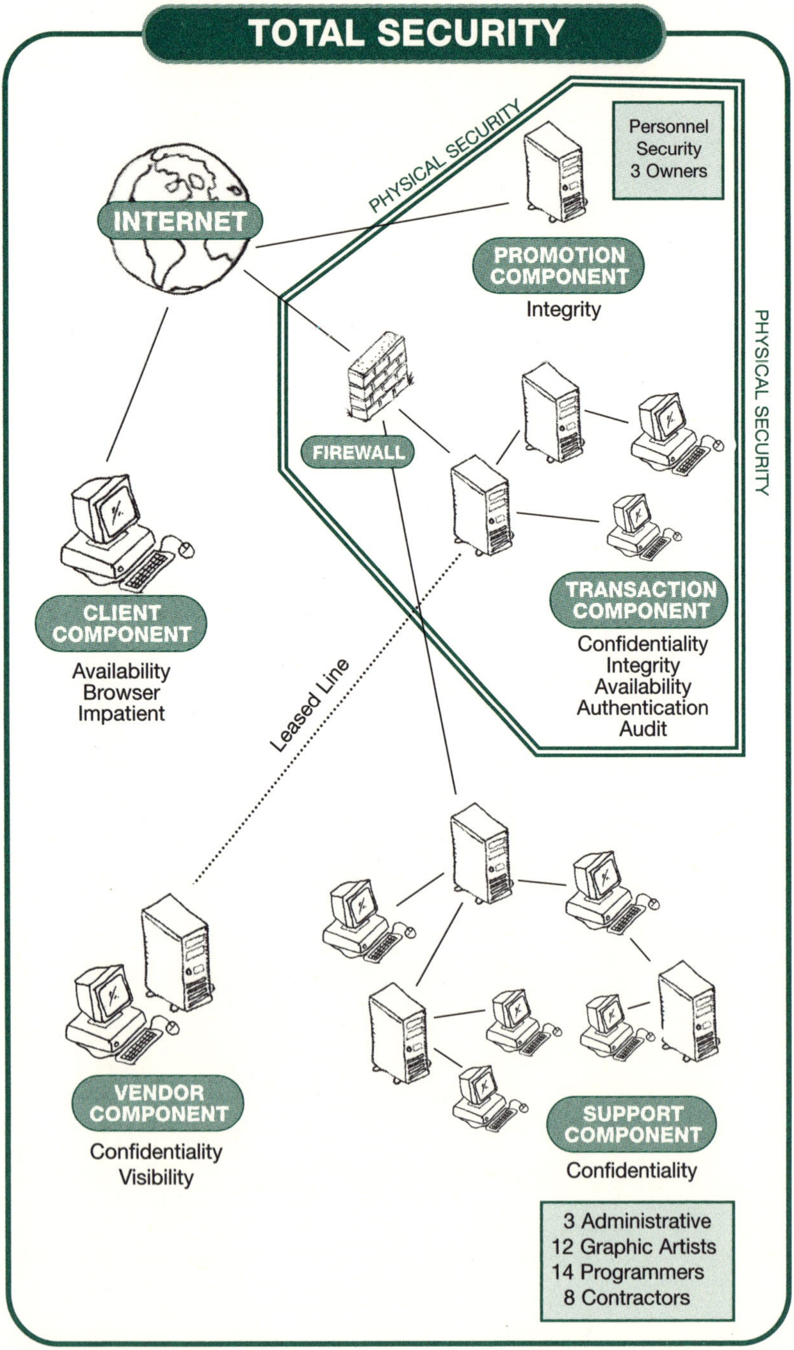
TOTAL SECURITY
PHYSICAL SECURITY
Personnel Security 3 Owners
INTERNET
PROMOTION COMPONENT
Integrity
PHYSICAL SECURITY
FIREWALL
TRANSACTION COMPONENT
Confidentiality
Integrity
Availability
Authentication
Audit
CLIENT COMPONENT
Availability
Browser
Impatient
Leased Line
VENDOR COMPONENT
Confidentiality
Visibility
SUPPORT COMPONENT
Confidentiality
3 Administrative
12 Graphic Artists
14 Programmers
8 Contractors

"How are we going to fix *that* problem?" Kris said.

"Didn't you say that you were going to expand and take over the restaurant space next door?"

"Yes, in a couple of weeks."

"Well, the good news is that restaurant kitchens typically have cinderblock firewalls that extend from the building's floor to the real roof, to prevent a kitchen fire from traveling over walls like these into other areas of the building."

"Ok, I got it, but even so, we can't fit *all* of our computers in that small space," Kris said.

"You don't have to put all the computers in there."

Sean quickly leaned forward and said, "I've got it!"

"From your napkin analysis, we only need to protect five of our computers, the ones that support the Promotion and Transaction functions. Five computers, our uninterrupted power supply, firewall, routers, switches and modems will all fit in that kitchen space."

"Also, the room is already alarmed because presently they secure the cash and valuables there," Kris added, "and there is fire suppression built in. We'll have to check to see if it's the right kind for computers, but basically I think all we will have to do is wall up the serving door behind the counter."

"That will cut down on the expenses of securing the room," added Kris.

"Spoken like a real entrepreneur, soda anyone?" Phil replied.

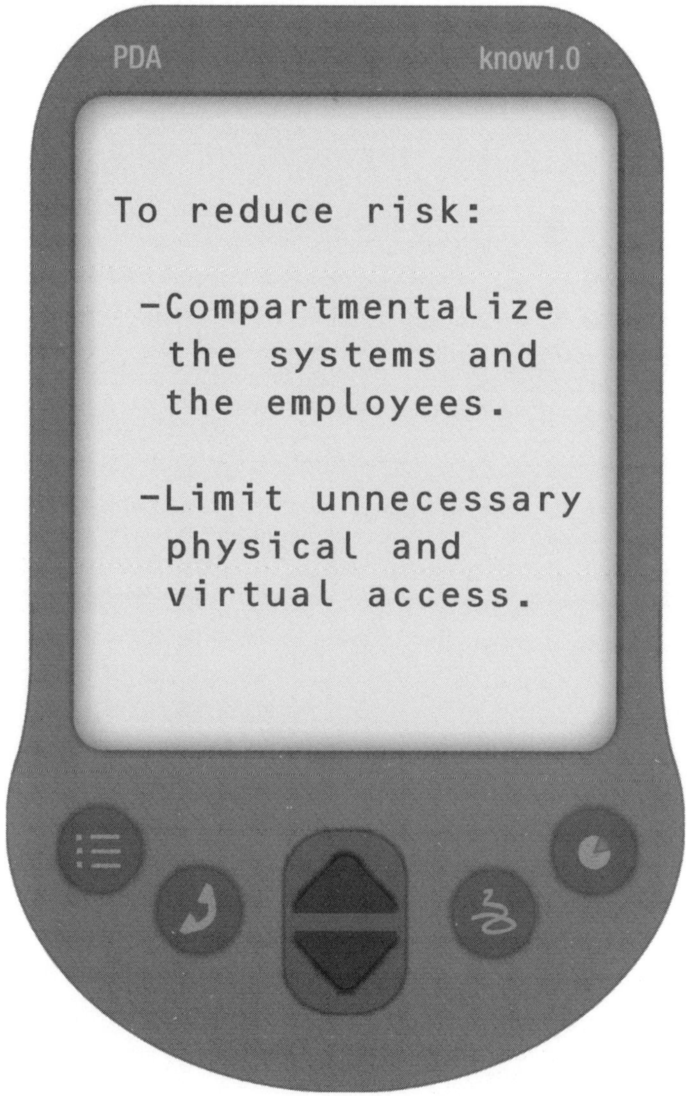
PDA
know1.0
To reduce risk:
-Compartmentalize the systems and the employees.
-Limit unnecessary physical and virtual access.

The Cashier Cage

"OK, while we are on the subject of firewalls, you also need to get a good network firewall to support your Internet connections. Although the one you currently have is adequate, you need a better one," said Phil.

Terry added, "The reason you need a firewall on your system is because you deploy a lot of software, commercial and your own, which often has security vulnerabilities. A good firewall provides a trusted software and/or hardware interface that doesn't allow internal and external entities to gain access to those vulnerabilities on your system."

"Entities?" asked Paula.

"Sorry. I mean things like people and software applications," Terry clarified.

"Terry's correct. Current statistics show that every three months hundreds of new software vulnerabilities are identified. Why is this? Think about the software that you use to send e-mail: Simple Message Transfer Protocol or SMTP. Well, there's nothing simple about SMTP, it has hundreds of thousands of lines of code and is developed by programmers all over the world. These programmers are focused on building new functionality, not creating minimal or secure software, so how good can that be for security?

"As you know, a firewall is basically a computer with networking cards or modems so it can be installed between several networks. The difference between a firewall and a normal computer is that the only software on the firewall is what is needed to run the firewall operations. Even the operating system has any unneeded code removed. That way if a new vulnerability is discovered in that extra code, you don't have to worry about it. Also, they close all the known holes and vulnerabilities in the firewall.

"Now, I said *known* holes and vulnerabilities. It's very important that you install all the security product updates to protect against all of the new holes and attacks."

Kris thought for a moment, "Do the security vendors make many mistakes in developing their products?"

"Not intentionally," Phil quipped, "In the early 1990's, I know of a group of security professionals who worked hard to build a very strong firewall for the military.

"They did lots of things to ensure that the system would refuse unauthorized access to classified information. Finally, an independent, third-party group of eight highly qualified security experts verified that the system could be trusted to do only that. They did that by conducting code reviews and extensive security tests. Once they felt comfortable, they approved it."

"Even with all that, a year later the developers found a major hole in the system," Phil continued, "Not because they were sloppy, it was a new kind of attack."

"So it's not always bad product development," Phil finished, "You just need to ensure that you continue to get and install product updates immediately."

"Now I understand." Kris said.

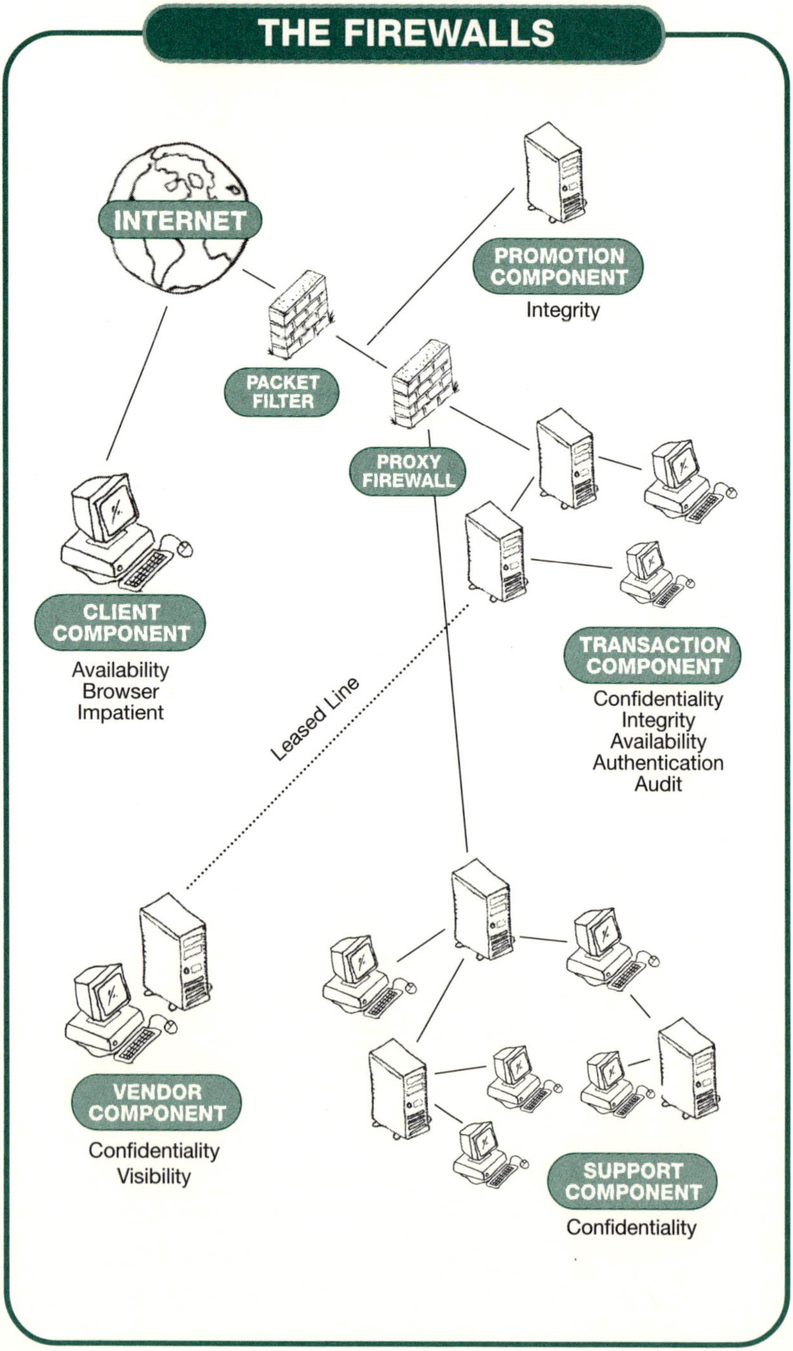
THE FIREWALLS
INTERNET
PROMOTION COMPONENT
Integrity
PACKET FILTER
PROXY FIREWALL
CLIENT COMPONENT
Availability
Browser
Impatient
TRANSACTION COMPONENT
Confidentiality
Integrity
Availability
Authentication
Audit
Leased Line
VENDOR COMPONENT
Confidentiality
Visibility
SUPPORT COMPONENT
Confidentiality

“Right! Now, let’s get back to the firewall. You need a packet filter as your first line of defense for all of your on-site components, and a proxy firewall to protect the individual security requirements of the Transaction and Support components.”

“What is the difference between the packet filter and the proxy firewall?” asked Kris.

“A **packet filter** is kind of like having a screened-in porch, you can see people passing and they can see you, but it filters out the bugs. A **proxy firewall** is like a locked door and a mean dog to protect the house from burglars. The key to the door and the dog verify and allow authorized people access to the inside.

The packet filter is very efficient and fast because it prevents undesirable packets from entering the network, like ones that are malicious or are not supported by your systems. The proxy firewall restricts traffic based on the characteristics of the communication protocol using software applications called proxies. The **proxies** can be configured to allow authorized entities to use a limited set of features provided by the larger software programs, like SMTP, without allowing them full access to the vulnerabilities in those programs.

“You see, the proxies have about 3,000 to 6,000 lines of code, which are easily designed, reviewed, and tested to ensure they have no vulnerabilities. Understand?” asked Phil.

“I think I do,” responded Kris still processing this new information.

"Let me provide you with an analogy. Basically, proxies are like the cashier in a casino's casher cage. Casinos don't let you walk into the cashier cage to withdraw, change, or deposit your cash and chips on your own. They make you work through the cashier, who verifies that you have an account, that you are who you say you are, and that the casino chips and cash are valid. Once all of that is verified, they transfer the money.

"The casino trusts the cashiers because they are trained, tested, and bonded. The casino also audits them, and the surveillance personnel watch them."

Phil noticed a look of surprise from the group. "What? You thought the cameras were only watching the players?" he asked.

"We don't anymore," responded Kris.

"How do we know which firewalls are good?" Sean asked.

"Personally, I would recommend that you get one that was developed by a company with a reputation for building IT security solutions and depends on that security reputation to maintain its business.

"You can also gain some assurance from security testing done by third-party certified labs."

Tap, tap, tap…

"Not just the marketing literature and the word of the firewall salesperson?" Kris asked innocently.

Everyone turned to her in unison. Smiling she said, "Just joking. Coffee anyone?"

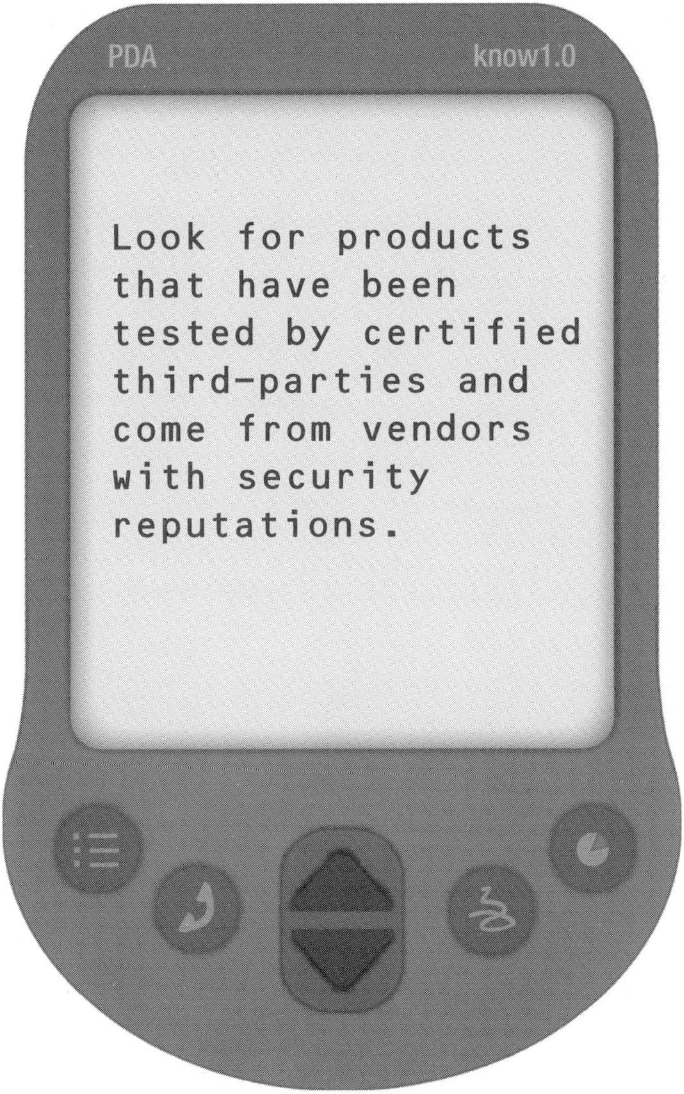
PDA
know1.0
Look for products that have been tested by certified third-parties and come from vendors with security reputations.

The Secure Tubes

When Phil and Kris came back with the coffee, Sean began, "Now for the hard questions. How do we authenticate the gamblers and protect the casinos' information as it passes over the Internet?"

"First," began Phil, "let's talk about authentication for both gamblers and casinos. We all know that static passwords are very weak. The good ones are so complicated and not user-friendly that they are usually written down by the users, making them vulnerable to prying eyes. Besides, they can still be intercepted as they are passed over the Internet and other systems. The best passwords are dynamic passwords."

"**Dynamic passwords**?" asked Sean.

"Dynamic means there is a different password for every time you login. If the user writes it down or someone was to copy the password, it will not work on the next login attempt," explained Terry.

"Sounds secure, but worse than the static option for the users," responded Sean.

"Luckily, dynamic authentication solutions have come a long way," Phil said, "we now have our pick of dynamic password technologies, challenge-and-response, time-based, and one-time passwords. They also come in various forms, like smart cards, USB tokens, PCMCIA cards, software programs, and credit card-size calculators."

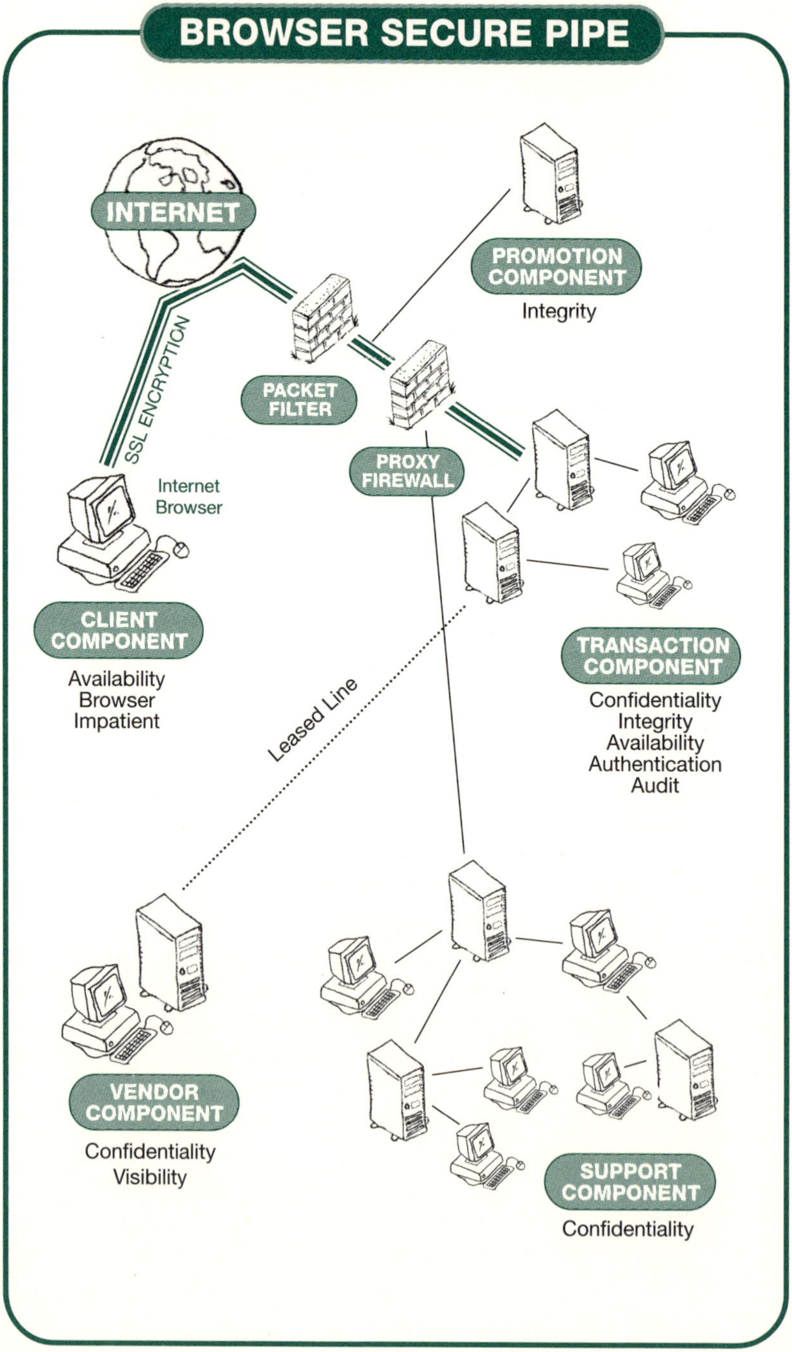
BROWSER SECURE PIPE
INTERNET
SSL ENCRYPTION
PACKET FILTER
PROXY FIREWALL
PROMOTION COMPONENT
Integrity
Internet Browser
CLIENT COMPONENT
Availability
Browser
Impatient
Leased Line
TRANSACTION COMPONENT
Confidentiality
Integrity
Availability
Authentication
Audit
VENDOR COMPONENT
Confidentiality
Visibility
SUPPORT COMPONENT
Confidentiality

"The problem is, as you have identified, your gamblers are impulse buyers and when they get to your site they want to gamble immediately. So they will not be willing to wait a couple of weeks for something like an authentication token to come in the mail.

"With all that in mind, we recommend that you use what the gamblers have readily available in their browsers, namely the SSL encryption and that they login with a static password of their choosing."

"**SSL?**" asked Kris.

"**Secure Socket Layer** encryption. You've seen it work when you connect to a website to make a financial purchase. Just before you buy something, you see a picture of a key or lock at the bottom of your browser screen," explained Sean.

"Correct. Basically, the gambler's browser and the vendor's transaction server jointly establish a virtual secure tube through the Internet by encrypting everything going from one to the other."

Kris added, "The little that I know about encryption is that we'll have to physically pass crypto keys from the browser to the server or the server to the browser, so wouldn't we be messing with the same client impatience problem?"

"Good question," replied Phil, "but the answer is no. SSL uses some very complex mathematical algorithms to securely exchange the crypto keys between the two systems over the Internet electronically. The user is never involved. No one can capture the crypto key in transit, and there is no waiting."

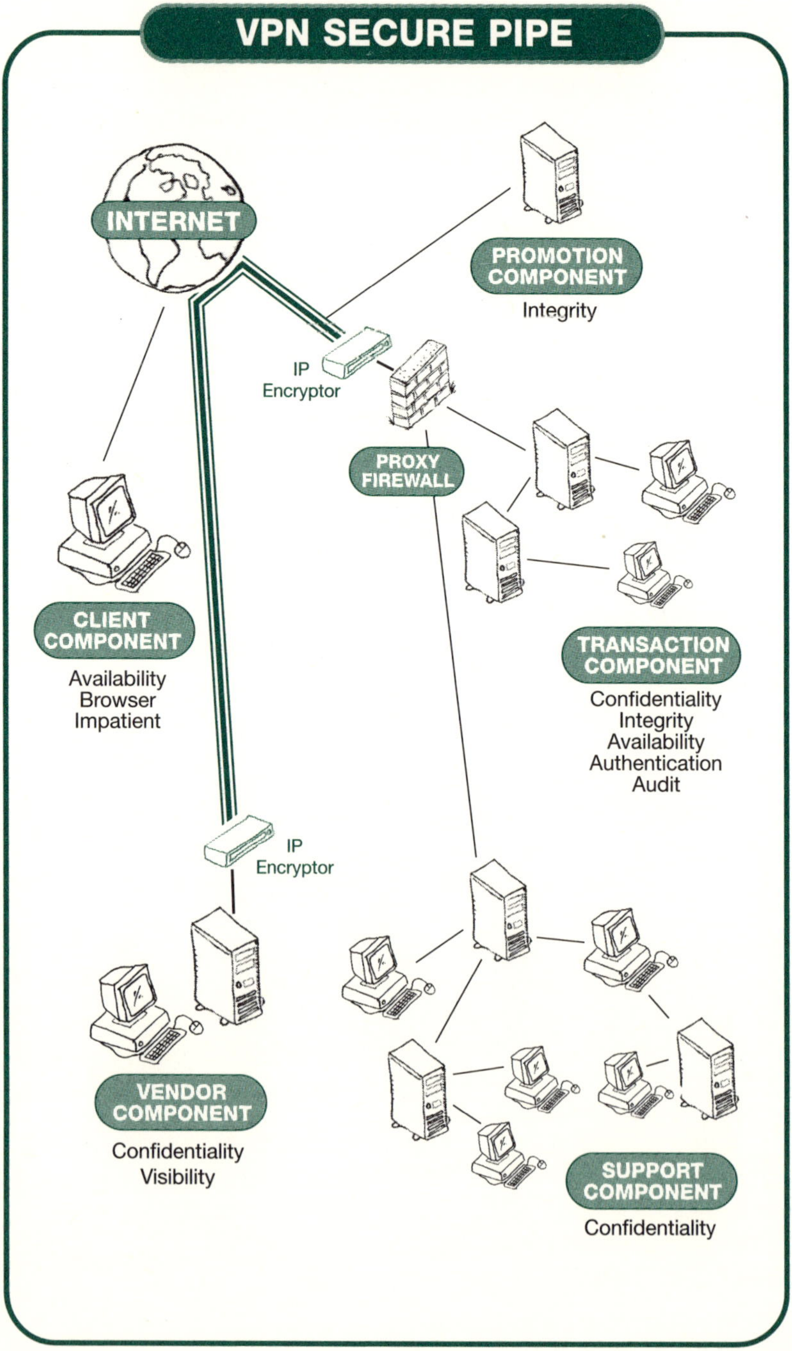
VPN SECURE PIPE
INTERNET
PROMOTION COMPONENT
Integrity
IP Encryptor
PROXY FIREWALL
CLIENT COMPONENT
Availability
Browser
Impatient
TRANSACTION COMPONENT
Confidentiality
Integrity
Availability
Authentication
Audit
IP Encryptor
VENDOR COMPONENT
Confidentiality
Visibility
SUPPORT COMPONENT
Confidentiality

"I see. So with this virtual secure tube, the client can pass their static encrypted password over the Internet and no one can read or copy it?" asked Kris.

"Correct. Also, all of their transactions will be more accurate and protected from eyes on the Internet."

"Can we use the same thing for the casinos?" asked Sean.

"Whoa! The casinos are not going to like being connected to the Internet," Kris exclaimed.

"She's right," Phil said, "We could use SSL, but the casinos have a different culture and requirements than their clients. Their visibility requirements demand a higher data through-put and they are not going to want the same connection to be used for surfing, email, or anything else on the Internet. Add that to their fear of **crackers,** or as some people call them, **hackers**, and you will have a hard time selling them on SSL. Isn't that why you're connected to them via leased lines?"

"*Expensive* leased lines," Kris corrected.

"That's great! It provides the perfect way to sell the casinos on connecting to the Internet. You and the casinos are going to like this solution a lot, because this is one of those situations where security is going to save you both a lot of money.

"Our recommendation is that you connect the casinos to the Transaction component via the Internet with IP encryptors at both ends."

Everyone looked at Phil and waited for a more detailed explanation.

"An **IP encryptor** is just a simple box. It makes information that goes out unreadable by encrypting it and de-encrypts whatever comes in, making the encrypted data readable.

"By placing an IP encryptor between your Transaction component and your Internet connection, and another one between the casino system and their Internet connection, you effectively create a secure tube between the two ends. This configuration ensures the confidentiality and integrity of the information as it passes over the Internet.

"And because each casino will have a different crypto key, it provides authentication. The maintenance is almost zero."

"I heard you say something about saving money and an easy sell to the casinos," Kris replied.

"Yes, this is the business part," said Phil, "What is the difference in paying for a leased line and an Internet connection?"

"$20,000 per month for the leased line and $6,000 per month for the Internet connection, so a $14,000 a month difference," Kris responded.

"At an initial cost of $2,000 per IP encryptor, or $4,000 per link, your **return-on-investment,** or **ROI,** is over 4,000% or $168,000 per casino in the first year. What CEO would not like to tell the stockholders about that in the annual report?"

"Wow! That's a record ROI for this company. With that, we are buying you two lunches. I think we can afford it with those savings!"

Tap, tap, tap...

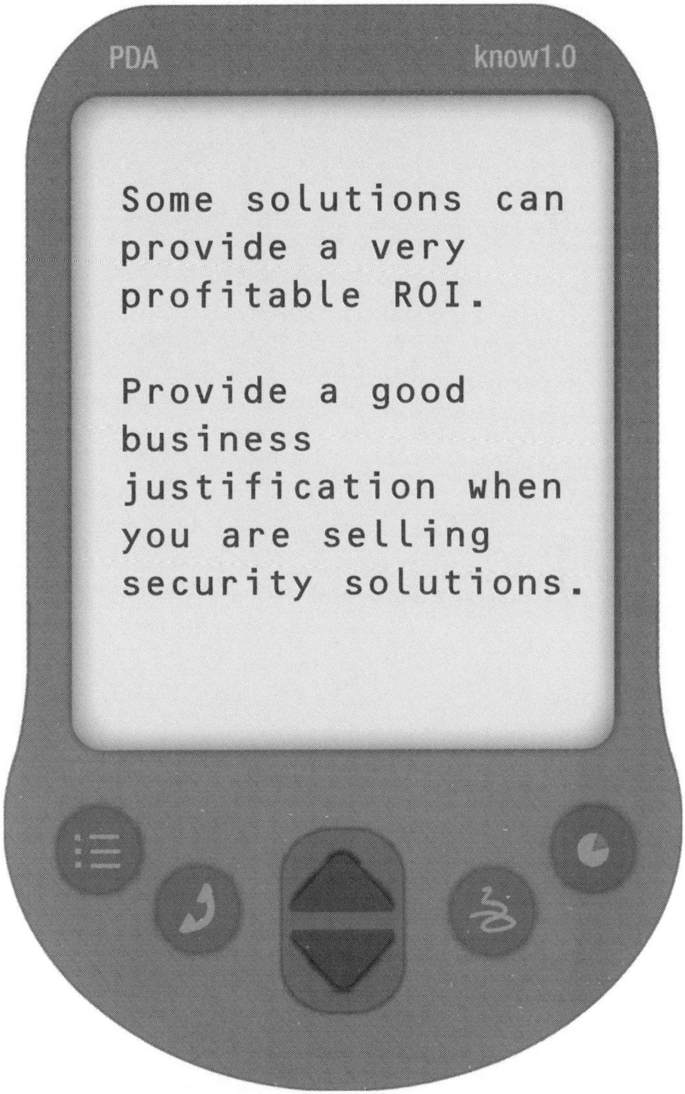
PDA
know1.0
Some solutions can provide a very profitable ROI.
Provide a good business justification when you are selling security solutions.

The Surveillance

The Tell
The Power Play
The Ace-in-the-Hole

The Tell

After lunch, everyone returned to the office and settled around the napkin drawing.

"Now that we've secured all the entry points," Phil proceeded, "you'll want to monitor how effective these points are to see if anything gets past your security."

"There are two monitoring solutions you should deploy, anti-virus and intrusion detection devices. Both work just like the casino surveillance operations. They look for player actions that indicate that someone may be cheating. The casinos call these actions, **tells**. The fact that a player is winning big is a tell to the casino operation that something is potentially wrong.

"An easy example of a tell in a casino is when someone is counting cards. Counting cards allows the player to identify when the deck favors the casino and when it favors them. Most players bet the same amount all the time, but when someone is counting cards, their bets are low when the deck is in the casino's favor, and their bets are high when the deck is in their favor. This is called bet variation. On computers and networks, cyber tells are virus signatures and attack profiles.

"You already have anti-virus software on all of your internal systems, so I would make two suggestions.

"One, update your anti-virus definitions twice a day on the Transaction and Promotion components, first thing in the morning and in the evening before you leave, and once a day on the Support component.

"New viruses are released every day and it's a lot simpler to update the definitions than it is to recover from an attack. The reason for different frequencies is you want to reduce the risk to your most critical systems supporting the Transaction and Promotion components."

Tap, tap, tap…

"Two, extend your anti-virus site license to include all of the computers at your employees' homes, since they work a lot at home and send or bring their programs into work on disks. Upgrading your license this way pushes your protection perimeter out farther."

"Extending the license is a small additional cost," Kris added, "and we could also promote it as an employee benefit."

Tap, tap, tap…

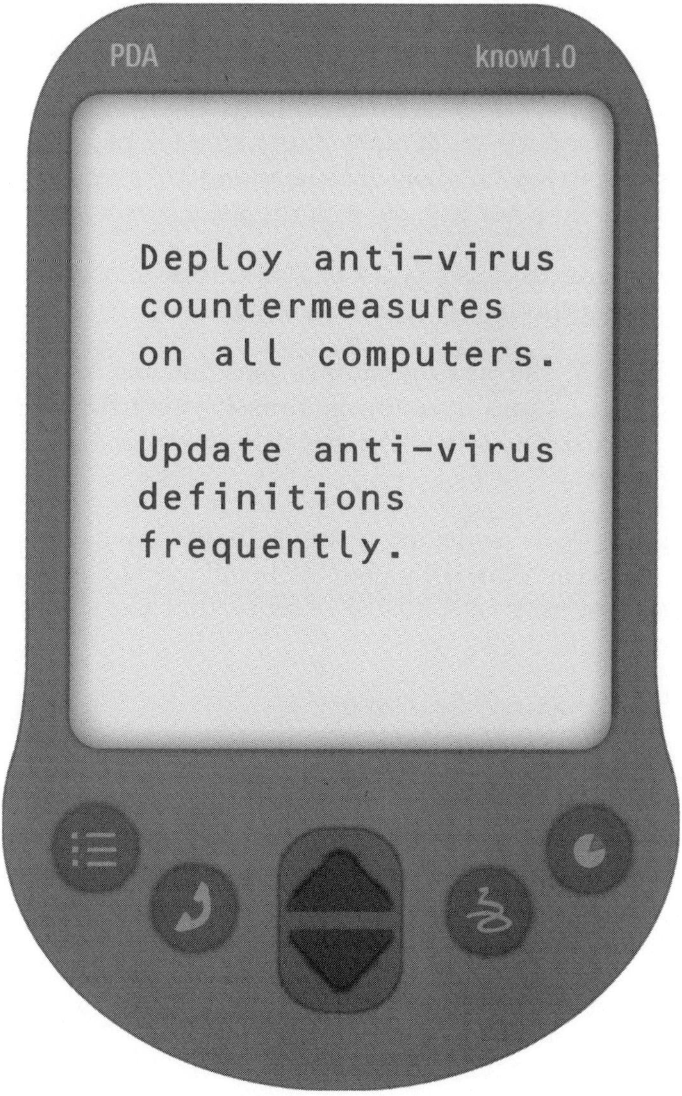

Deploy anti-virus countermeasures on all computers.

Update anti-virus definitions frequently.

"Now let's talk about **intrusion detection systems,** or **IDS's**. IDS's monitor the traffic that passes through the system and looks for inappropriate activities that match known attack profiles. When they find something suspicious, they alert someone.

"Think of the IDS as a little old lady who is sitting on her porch with a large set of binoculars and a telephone. All day long she watches for suspicious or interesting activities and reports them to her friends or to the police.

"There are two basic types of IDS's: **link** and **host.** Host IDS's are also referred to as a server IDS.

"A link IDS sits on a communications line and watches the traffic as it passes over the link, as if our little old lady's porch is in the middle of the street or overlooking a stretch of highway.

"A host IDS is loaded on a server to watch what happens on that server. This is like our little old lady overseeing an intersection. She sees all the activity that is moving from multiple links."

"Which is better?" Sean asked.

"It depends on the business, the system design and your goals. Primarily, you have to determine what the system's most critical components are and that is based on the business. In your case, this is the Transaction component, so I would recommend that you place a link IDS between the Transaction component and the firewall."

"Why not put it outside the firewall?" asked Kris.

"If you put it outside the firewall, you'll get alarms on all the attempted attacks on your system, including the ones the firewall stops. Unless you want to be responding to alarms all the time, I would put it inside the firewall."

"Don't IDS's have a reputation of producing a lot of false alarms?" Sean asked.

"Yes, and because of this a lot of people shut them off. To prevent that, you have to spend time in the beginning tailoring your IDS configuration for your specific operations or you'll be overloaded with false alerts.

"Accurate tailoring requires utilizing someone who is very knowledgeable of your systems, operations and the IDS. You can't just load it and turn it on."

Tap, tap, tap…

"So, we need to spend time tailoring and configuring the IDS to our operations or hire someone to answer alarms all day," Sean concluded.

"Correct. Let's take a break and get a cold drink from the grocery store next door."

As the group made their way to the door, suddenly everything shook and it became dark and quiet.

Terry, who was already out the door, immediately looked toward the volcano, relieved to see there was no change.

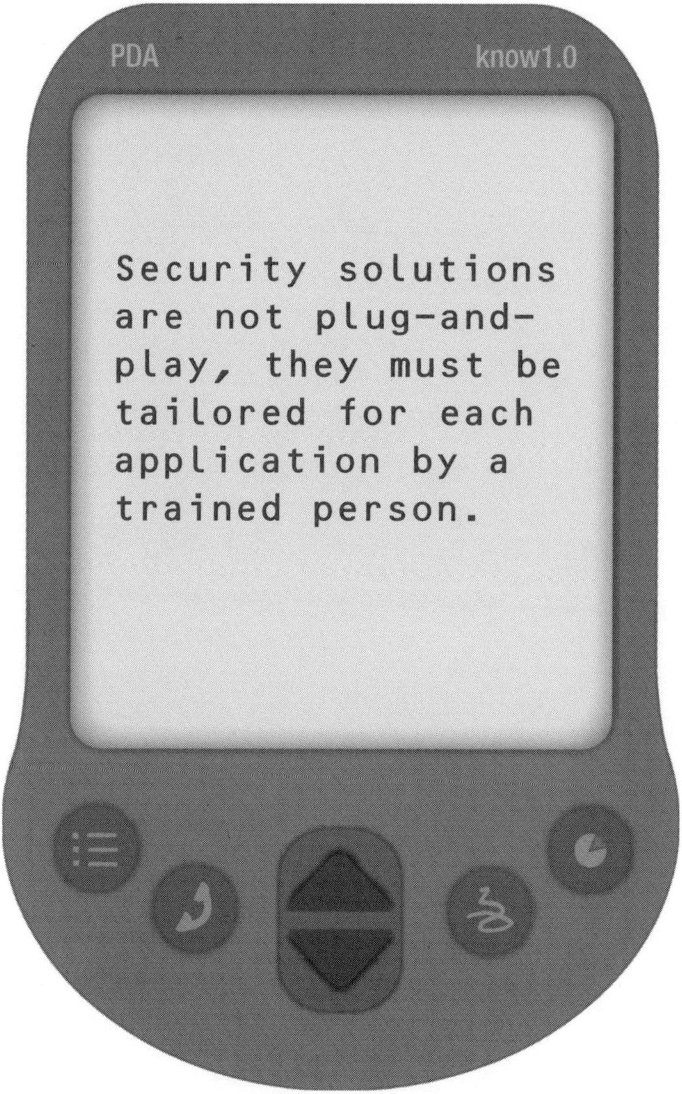
PDA
know1.0
Security solutions are not plug-and-play, they must be tailored for each application by a trained person.

The Power Play

It was a mild tremor, but enough to cause a loss of electrical power. The calypso music was silent, as was the constant hum from the air conditioners and computers.

"Terry, check the status of the Transaction components," Phil said.

Terry made a quick check.

"The Transaction components are running off of the UPS, so that should keep things going for about 10 to 20 minutes," Terry reported.

"Good." Phil replied, "How often do you lose power and how long does the normal outage last?"

Kris glanced at Sean. They were both silent. Finally Kris responded, "Two or three times a week. They usually last from 15 minutes to several hours."

"Hmm. That doesn't bode well for having the Transaction component at constant availability."

"We know. We've been talking about purchasing an emergency generator. We've put it off because the system, installation, and continuous maintenance are going to be a major cost," said Kris.

"That's true, but something will have to be done. There's nothing we can do now, but shut the system down and buy those drinks before they get warm."

They left the cool office and stepped out into the hot island air. Phil heard a familiar repetitive drumming sound.

"That's an emergency diesel generator running. Where is it?" he asked.

"It could be for the bank or the grocery store," replied Sean, "The dime store and the restaurant couldn't afford one."

"It has to be the grocery store, because it costs a lot of money when perishable food goes bad," Phil concluded, "Kris, come with me, we're going to buy the grocery store manager a cup of coffee."

An hour later, Kris and Phil returned to the stuffy, quiet, dark office with the backup power problem solved.

"Phil got us an emergency backup generator!" Kris announced.

"That fast? How much?" Sean asked.

"He talked the manager of the grocery store into letting us run an electrical extension cord from his generator to our Transaction component for $50 a month."

As an afterthought, Kris added, "But don't we have to worry about power surges when the generator kicks on?"

"Our UPS has a surge protector that will shield our systems from that," Sean replied.

"What about the rest of the computers?" Kris asked.

"Give the employees a security awareness presentation, have a technical discussion, read technical manuals, or have a corporate lunch. You have lots of options," responded Terry.

Surprised at this non-technical response from Terry, Phil said, "Very good, especially the awareness piece. It is always a good idea for management to promote the need for security on a frequent basis."

"Now, I have one more question to ask related to backups."

And with that – the lights, air conditioning, and calypso music returned to the office.

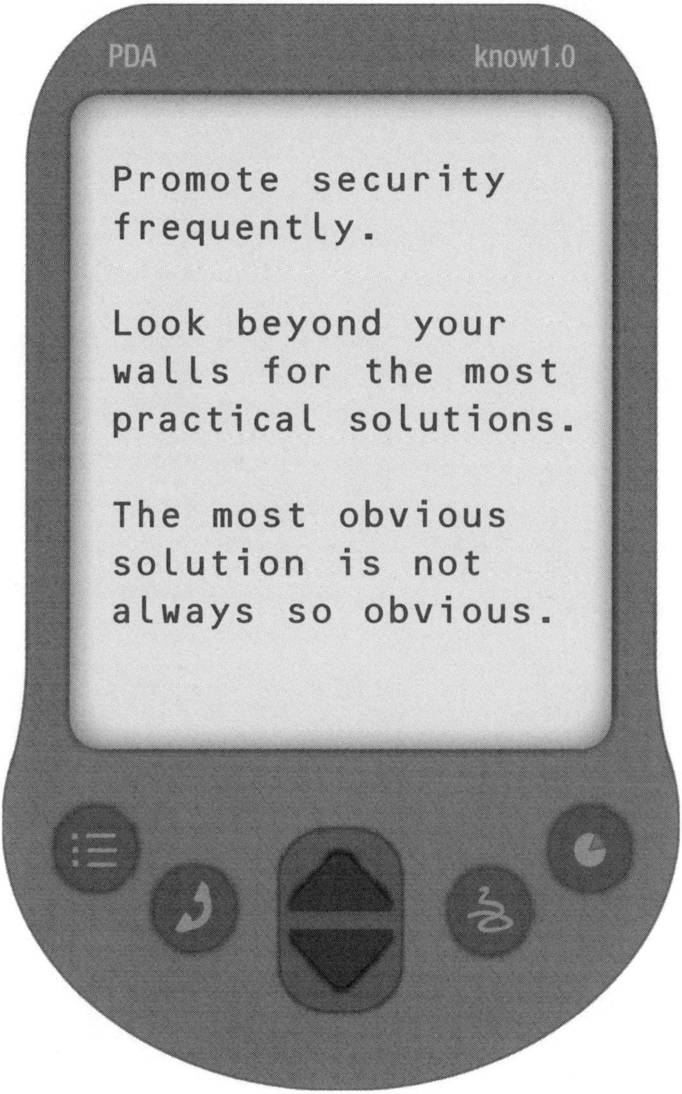
PDA
know1.0
Promote security frequently.
Look beyond your walls for the most practical solutions.
The most obvious solution is not always so obvious.

The Ace-in-the-Hole

Phil began, "No matter how many countermeasures you deploy, there is no such thing as zero risk security. Someday, something will happen that you didn't think about. Do you backup your systems' information to support your recovery operations?"

Sean was full of pride, "We do it every day and keep three days of backups: son, father and grandfather, or day one, day two and day three."

"And where do you store them?"

His eyes dropped to the floor as he pointed at a shelf in the room, "On the shelf over there."

"And if the building burns down…" Phil began.

"We understand. Yesterday our insurance representative told us that we needed a $2,000 fire-proof safe to protect them," Kris responded.

"Alright, Kris, where do you live?"

"I own a house on the other side of the island."

"What's the possibility of this building and your house burning down at the same time?"

Sean quickly said, "The island's volcano erupting would be the most likely."

Tap, tap – "Huh?!", Terry exclaimed.

Before Terry could respond any further, Kris cut in, "Let's all agree that if that volcano goes off we'll have bigger problems than worrying about this business."

"Hold on a sec," Phil exclaimed, "I feel a BFO moment coming on. I'm going to buy you an alternative to your $2,000 fire-proof safe. I'll be right back."

Phil returned from the grocery store with $21.49 in purchases. Terry was involved in a serious conversation with Sean about the risks of erupting volcanoes.

Kris met Phil in the middle of the room, followed by Sean, who was happy to change the subject of the volcano conversation. They were all looking at the bag in Phil's hands.

"Kind of small and light to be a $2,000 fire-proof safe," said Kris.

Phil pulled three six-pack soda coolers from the bag and with a black marker he numbered them '1', '2', and '3'. "There you go: day one, day two and day three, or son, father, and grandfather.

"Um, those will never survive a fire," Terry said, his thoughts never far from erupting volcanoes.

"They aren't for protecting the backups from fire. They're for transporting and storing them."

Kris proclaimed, "Now I'm having a BFO moment. You want me to take the new day's backups to my house for off-site storage. Now *that* is simple and effective!"

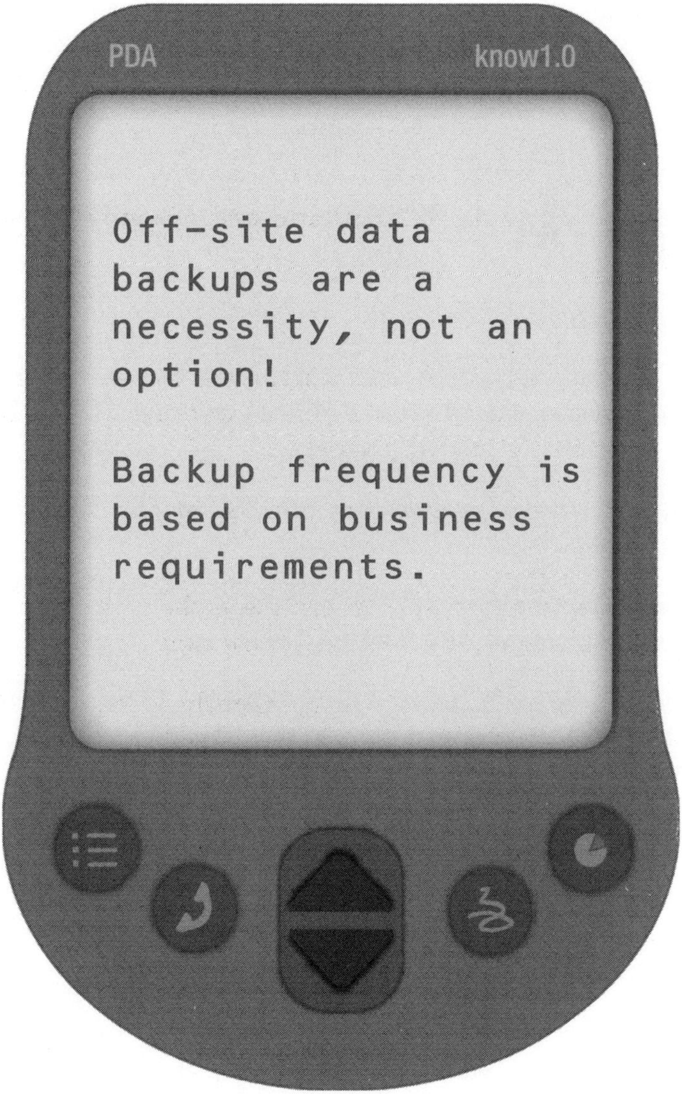
PDA
know1.0
Off-site data backups are a necessity, not an option!
Backup frequency is based on business requirements.

"I always follow the **'KISS Principle'**, **Keep IT Security Simple**."

Tap, tap, tap…

Phil pulled out a lock and latch from the shopping bag, "You'll lock the other two in a cabinet or closet at your home during the day for added protection."

"Clever. Drinks are on me tonight at the beach bar," announced Kris.

"I bet that tonight we can even see the glow from that volcano erupting on the horizon," Sean said.

Terry shook his head, shivering slightly, as he walked out the door into the tropical heat of the island.

PDA
know1.0
KISS Principle:
Keep
IT
Security
Simple

The End Game

The End Game

"What a fantastic visit," Kris began as she drove Phil and Terry to the airport, "After we left the bar last night, Sean and I talked about how much we've learned about IT security in such a short period of time."

"Better than taking a course in school," concurred Sean, who was along for the ride.

"That's because you were so open to new ideas, quick to comprehend the concepts and ready to apply them to your problem," Phil complimented them.

"Well, you also allowed us to come up with our own solutions which helped us understand and own them," Sean added.

"So what would you say was the most important thing that you learned?" Phil asked.

"Let me answer first," Sean started. "It was that security is based on the business requirements."

"Good!"

Tap, tap, tap…

Kris added, "If we had reviewed our business and security requirements together when we were initially designing our system, we would have saved a lot of time and money."

"Outstanding!"

Then Terry spoke up, "I learned that IT security is not just about technology. In fact, it is only about ten to twenty percent of the security solution."

"Excellent point! In fact, whenever I begin a system's security assessment, I review the **Nine P's**:

"**Profit** is where business drives the system's security policy and solutions.

"**Policy** is the basis for all security decisions.

"**Procedures**, **Physical**, **Personnel** and **Product**, or technology, are the sources of the majority of the security solutions.

"**Promotion** informs everyone of what their responsibilities are related to supporting security and of management's emphasis on the need for security.

"**Plan** for recovery when the system comes under attack and the deployed security is not enough.

"**Practical** is the key to good security, because if the security solutions are too cumbersome they will be neither used nor effective."

Tap, tap, tap…

"Well, we're here. Since we have plenty of time to check in, we'd like to buy you two your last cups of island-brewed coffee in the airport cafe," Kris announced.

Turning to Phil, Terry asked, "Do you mean that we're never coming back to the island?" As an afterthought, he looked at them, "I mean, as beautiful as it is, I'm happy to leave the erupting volcanoes."

Kris replied "You have both taught us well, so I figure your odds are pretty good that you will not be returning."

"*Really* good," added Phil, "but don't worry about the volcano, because I did a little risk assessment on that, and the odds of it erupting while we were here are more than a million to one."

"Really? I was so focused on fearing the volcano that I forgot to do a risk assessment on the probability of the volcano erupting. What a fool I've been," Terry said shaking his head.

"You're not alone. Many IT managers are so fearful of IT security that they never conduct an IT security assessment," responded Phil.

"Reviewing what I've learned during this IT security assessment, I can personally say that our assessment has increased my ability to effectively and efficiently manage this operation," said Kris.

"You have replaced my FUD perspective with an increased understanding of my IT system's critical components and security options. It has really improved my job, because I now know when and how to respond to specific IT system problems," she continued.

Tap, tap, tap…

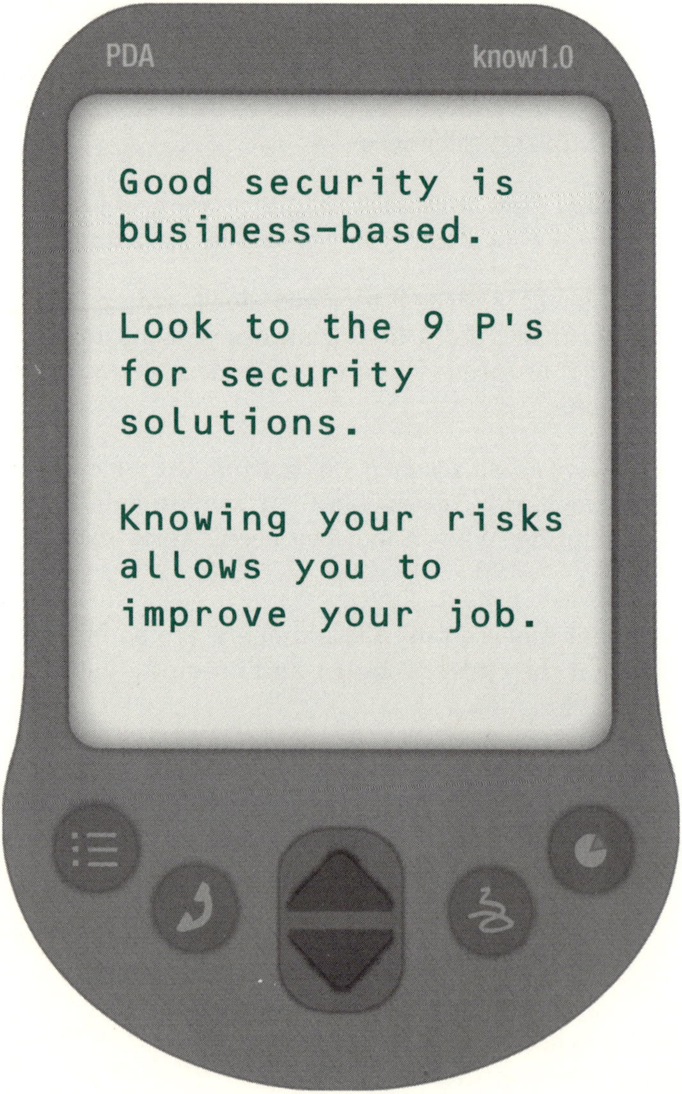
PDA
know1.0
Good security is business-based.
Look to the 9 P's for security solutions.
Knowing your risks allows you to improve your job.

"Good. If more managers understood that reality, they would be asking for security assessments," responded Phil.

"If more security experts approached security from a business perspective, managers would be more supportive of their security requests," added Kris.

"When you want to work with others, it helps if you understand their culture, language, and motivations," Phil said.

"And that you're warned about the pepper sauce!" Terry concluded.

Acronyms

BFO	Blinding Flash of the Obvious
B.S.	Business-based Security
CIAAA	Confidentiality, Integrity, Availability, Authentication, and Audit
FUD	Fear, Uncertainty, and Doubt
IDS	Intrusion Detection System
IP	Internet Protocol
IT	Information Technology
PCMCIA	Personal Computer Memory Card International Association
PDA	Personal Digital Assistant
ROI	Return-On-Investment
SMTP	Simple Mail Transfer Protocol
SSL	Secure Socket Layer
UPS	Uninterrupted Power Supply
USB	Universal Serial Bus
VPN	Virtual Private Network

Author's Comments

KNOW IT Security is loosely based on a security assessment of an Internet gambling casino that I supervised several years ago. The characters are fictional, but the attitudes, concepts, misperceptions, strategies, and solutions were from my personal experiences while participating in IT security assessments over the past twenty-five years.

The three main concepts that I have learned are:

- good security decisions are based on the organization's mission or business.

- the most practical security solutions are a combination of all the security disciplines, not just technology.

- IT systems can never be totally secure – there will always be residual risk, so always have a recovery plan.

As a writer, I hope that I have presented these concepts to you in manner that was understandable, informative, relevant, and entertaining.

About the Author

James P. Litchko is a senior information systems security author and strategic advisor. He has over twenty-five years experience assessing and developing information technology (IT) security solutions. He has held senior executive positions and advised executive at several of the largest commercial IT security companies. During his twenty-year Naval career, as a surface warfare and cryptographic officer, he spent twelve years supporting operations in the Atlantic, Pacific, European, and Middle Eastern theaters. His last five years in the Navy were in staff and technical positions at the National Security Agency (NSA) and the National Computer Security Center (NCSC), where he was Staff Chief for the Director. Since 1988, he has been an instructor for computer and network security at Johns Hopkins University, the MIS Training Institute, and the National Cryptologic School. He has been a keynote speaker, presenter, and facilitator at over 30 events a year and a professional member of the National Speakers' Association. He has provided IT security presentations to Congressional staffs, Gartner Group, Conference Board, Canadian Embassy and Communications Security Establishment, Price Waterhouse, Merck, Exxon, Freddie Mac, Cambridge University, University of Mexico, SANS Institute, Computer Security Institute, Defense Intelligence University, and National Defense University. He has served on several government-sponsored, IT security working groups and was the past Chair of the ASIS International IT Security Council. A student of Ken Blanchard, Ph.D., author of *The One-Minute Manager®*, he holds a Masters degree in Information Systems from John Hopkins University and a Bachelors degree in Industrial Technology from Ohio University. He has authored or co-authored the following books: *KNOW Your Life*, *KNOW IT Security*, and *KNOW Cyber Risk*. Additionally, he is provides management, business development, and strategic planning support for high-tech start-up companies.

Special Thanks

KNOW IT Security couldn't have been completed without the special help from friends and associates. The support and encouragement they provided was truly commendable. Thanks for the initial edit of the book by Erin Sexton and special thanks to Kristin Adolfson for the final edit, formatting, and publishing of ***KNOW IT Security***. Finally to my lovely bride Jane, who provided me with the critical inputs on the many drafts and supported my hours, days, weeks, and months locked in my office and on travel working to develop this book.

INDEX

Other Books by Author Jim Litchko

KNOW Cyber Risk – By Managing your IT Security!

KNOW Cyber Risk is a story about an IT manager who identifies successful strategies for common issues surrounding security assessments. This book provides business professionals, IT managers, and IT security specialists with a quick, informal, and entertaining introduction to successful strategies for:

- ***making IT security decisions*** based on business needs.
- ***selling IT security*** solutions and justifications to senior management.
- ***motivating operational managers*** to request IT security assessments.
- ***understanding the complex security concepts*** of risk assessments.

Learn how to apply real-world and practical business goals to security, gain managerial control of risk assessments, and develop a collaborative strategy for company wide security practices.

*"**KNOW Cyber Risk** is a must read for all those managers that have IT systems supporting their business. Jim and Al have effectively introduced effective strategies on how to approach a security assessment and sell their bosses on security."*

— The Honorable Arthur L. Money, former Assistant Secretary of Defense for Command, Control, Communications and Intelligence, Department of Defense

KNOW **Your Life – By Organizing It!**

Become more effective and efficient in managing and organizing your life while saving time, gaining control over demands, and increasing your confidence in handling crisis situations. ***KNOW Your Life*** condenses all your records and personal documents into one place and serves as a reference that quickly supports you, your partner, or your loved ones during everyday tasks or in times of crisis. You will gain the tools to organize your:

- ***Personal Identity***: birth certificates, passports, drivers licenses…
- ***Income:*** employment, retirement, social security…
- ***Finances:*** bank accounts, credit cards…
- ***Investments:*** stocks, bonds…
- ***Properties:*** house, timeshares, cars, boats…
- ***Insurance:*** life, property, car…
- ***Health:*** medial plans, hospitals, doctors…
- ***Wishes:*** wills, arrangements, notifications…

*"**Know Your Life** is a wonderful personal and financial resource that everyone should own and use, whether single, newlywed, or married for 50 years. We urge our clients to seek out this great handbook."*

— R. Robert Goldman, Chief Investment Officer, Banneker Capital Management Corp.

QUICK ORDER FORM

Give the gift of ***KNOW IT Security*** to colleagues, managers, or security professionals.

	QTY	TOTAL
KNOW Cyber Risk for $14.95 USD each	_______	$__________
KNOW IT Security for $14.95 USD each	_______	$__________
Sales tax: Maryland residents add 5% sales tax	**MD Tax**	$__________
Shipping costs: Include $3.75 USD shipping & handling for first book and $3.00 for each additional book.	**Shipping**	$__________
	TOTAL	$__________

❑ **YES!** I am interested in having James P. Litchko speak or give a seminar at my company, association, school, or organization. Please send me more information.

Please allow 3 weeks for delivery after publication.

Payment: Payment must accompany orders. Make check or money order payable to ***Know Book Publishing***, or complete the following credit card information and sign:

Please charge my: ❑ VISA ❑ MASTERCARD ❑ AMERICAN EXPRESS

BILLING INFORMATION	**SHIPPING ADDRESS** ❑ same as billing
Name: ____________________	Name: ____________________
Organization: ____________________	Address Line1: ____________________
Address: ____________________	Address Line2: ____________________
City/State/Zip: ____________________	City/State/Zip: ____________________
Phone: ____________________	E-mail: ____________________
Card Number: ____________________	Name On Card: ____________________
Exp. Date: ____________________	Signature: ____________________

Fax orders: 240-363-0231. Send this completed form. Credit card orders only.

Web orders: Visit http://www.knowbookpublishing.com to order via the Internet.

Postal orders: Mail this completed form to:

Know Book Publishing
P.O. Box G
Kensington, MD. 20895